A FLIGHT AGAINST ALL ODDS

SCOTLAND TO AUSTRALIA IN 1968

Kate Clements

(formerly Kathy Wright)

Published in Australia by Sid Harta Publishers Pty Ltd,
ABN: 46 119 415 842
23 Stirling Crescent, Glen Waverley, Victoria 3150 Australia
Telephone: +61 3 9560 9920, Facsimile: +61 3 9545 1742
E-mail: author@sidharta.com.au

First published in Australia 2014
This edition published August 2014

Cover design, typesetting: Chameleon Print Design

Disclaimer

These memoirs (copyright) are an authentic, factual, unabridged and unembellished record of the flight from Scotland to Australia in a single engine aircraft, and represent the opinion and experience of events by the author as detailed in her diary during the journey.

Every effort has been made to acknowledge and contact the copyright holders for their permission to reproduce newspaper and photographic material contained in this book. Where the attempt to get permission has been unsuccessful, the author would be pleased to hear from the copyright owner so that any omission or error can be rectified.

If, while writing her memoirs, the author has misrepresented events, interactions, or situations it is purely through her limited knowledge and lack of political awareness, combined with the extreme pressures she faced at that time.

Further, if any persons named in the memoirs feel as if they have been misrepresented or maligned it has not been done with malicious intent, rather it is a reflection on how the author, as a 24 year old construed the circumstances to be at that time in 1968.

Clements, Kate
A Flight Against All Odds:
Scotland to Australia in 1968
ISBN: 1-922086-31-2
EAN13: 978-1-922086-31-0
pp280

About the author

Kate is a fit and healthy, seventy-year-old retiree, living in Adelaide, South Australia, very much enjoying the free time for travelling, reading, walking, swimming and learning *Tai Chi*. She is an active member of the International Lions Club of Burnside, giving something worthwhile back to the community.

Kate was born Kathleen Anne White in Lincoln, England, in 1944, the youngest of four children. In 1946, the family moved to Glasgow, Scotland, where she had a middle-class, well-disciplined upbringing. At the age of eighteen she met George Wright and they married six years later in 1968.

In Australia, after the birth of her two sons and a daughter in the 1970s, Kate gained qualifications through the Technical and Further Education college and university, which enabled her to establish a long and highly successful career in the vocation of children's services, care and education. She holds passionate beliefs regarding the "rights of the child" and the need to strengthen public awareness about child protection and domestic violence.

Kate and George divorced in 1998 and both have since remarried. Kate is now married to Glen Clements and has eight grandchildren and three step-grandchildren.

Kate became an Australian citizen in 1988 and has since made three trips back to Scotland by conventional commercial air travel to visit family and friends. However, she greatly appreciates the opportunities and lifestyle that Australia has given her and she very much regards this wonderful country as her home.

Whereas she has absolutely no regrets about her decision to join George on that 1968 flight from Scotland to Australia, the very stressful nature of those four months took a profound emotional toll. So much so that Kate was unable to revisit the diary she had written en route until much later in life. However, with the encouragement of family and friends Kate has finally overcome those apprehensions and documented the epic adventure in *A Flight Against All Odds: Scotland to Australia in 1968.*

Acknowledgements

First and foremost I must acknowledge the pilot, George Wright, without whom this epic adventure from Scotland to Australia would not have taken place. His skills as a private pilot and "fixer" were without question. We would never have achieved the outcome we did, had it not been for his Scottish tenacity, hot-headed determination, ability to find solutions when all else seemed lost and at times, his abrasive and confrontational manner.

After all these years, I am pleased at last to have the opportunity to acknowledge and thank all those people who opened their homes and hearts for us. They generously gave us food and shelter and, when most needed, friendship, expert advice and encouragement. These kind people from all countries, creeds and walks of life, contributed greatly to our success. Without a doubt, the outcomes for George and I would have been vastly different had it not been for their intervention.

I would also like to acknowledge those who have assisted and supported me on this latest journey of having these memoirs published.

Finally, I must give recognition and heartfelt thanks to my husband, Glen, who has had the hardest job of all. Apart from assisting with the tedious and exacting job of editing, he has provided emotional support, encouraging me to persevere during those times when all seemed "too hard" and I was ready to "pack it in". His faith in my ability has never wavered and for this I am extremely grateful.

Dedication

For my grandchildren, Ashley, Crystal, Tjana, Isaac,
Mason, Stephan, Abigel, and Oliver.

Enjoy life, broaden your horizons and believe in your dreams

Have the confidence, strength of character, courage,
and tenacity to fulfil those dreams.

Our journey is your heritage.

Contents

Chapter 1

The Birth of an Adventure

Golf Alpha Sierra Charlie Golf — 'Charlie Golf'

At 07.37 on the morning of 19 June, 1968, a somewhat inexperienced twenty-eight year old pilot and an even less experienced twenty-four year old navigator took off from Turnhouse Aerodrome, Edinburgh, on the first stage of a journey that was scheduled to take six weeks. They were solemnly farewelled by the small group of family and friends gathered round the tiny aircraft sitting on the tarmac. Piled on the rear seat of the aircraft was one small suitcase of clothes and a few personal necessities, along with a large cardboard box containing thirty-three topographical maps. The rest of the paraphernalia required for flight and navigation purposes was placed safely on the front dashboard ready for use. The arsenal of luggage included a camera and an 8mm movie camera.

For the enthusiasts, the aircraft in question was a three-seater Beagle Terrier (similar to an Auster) with a wooden propeller and a tail wheel. The body and wings were constructed of canvas stretched over a metal frame, while the engine was encased in a metal cowling. It had a Gypsy Major Ten four-stroke engine that could run on filtered petrol (common car fuel) if avgas (aviation fuel) was unavailable. But I must introduce myself and start the story from the beginning.

—

All those years ago I was known as Kathy Wright. My real name is Kathleen or Kate to family and close friends, but at the age of twenty-four, 'Kate' was not cool, so I chose to be known as Kathy. I was engaged to George — William George Wright. George was a motor mechanic by trade with experience in managing pubs. In 1967, George and his brother bought and renovated old style apartments for a living, converting them to single room flats for student accommodation.

—

The adventure had its beginnings in November of 1967.

—

Following six years of courtship, George and I set April 1968 as the date to marry. As the wedding date drew closer, we tried desperately to buy a house in Glasgow that would suit our everyday needs and allow us to run a business from the premises. Every time we put in a bid for a property our offer was upstaged. The constant disappointments experienced with this process left us quite despondent.

—

One morning in December, while driving through Glasgow,

George happened to see a poster advertising an information session and documentary, show-casing the benefits of migrating to Australia. Taking the attitude that it couldn't do any harm, he decided to attend. Being very much aware that the Australian Public Relations Department showed only the cream of its country's lure, George was not altogether impressed with the presentation. He did, however, concede that Australia could offer more than Scotland for a young, newly married couple starting a life together.

—

During the weeks that followed, there were many family discussions about George's employment prospects if we decided to pack up and go to the other side of the world.

With the little knowledge we had of Australia at that time, we concluded that the most valuable and beneficial training and experience he could have would involve flying light aircraft; something George had always wanted to do.

It never occurred to any of us what these kitchen table discussions would eventually lead to.

George decided to look into obtaining a private pilot's licence and, in February 1968, he enrolled in the Edinburgh Aero Club situated on the perimeter of Edinburgh Turnhouse Airport. It was while he was undertaking those first hours of flying tuition that the idea first came to him. Could he buy an aircraft and fly it to Australia himself? If this was possible, perhaps he could start his own business out there using his own aircraft.

Gradually this crazy idea gathered momentum. A world map was produced and the logistics of being able to fly to Australia in a series of short hops began to materialise.

At this point George couched the idea with his flying instructor, Ian Cooper, and Wing Commander, Jock Dalgleish. Wing Commander Dalgleish was a much respected and knowledgeable member of the Edinburgh Aero Club, having taught King Hussein of Jordan to fly, and having been the king's chief pilot for many years. Much to George's amazement, neither Ian nor Jock Dalgleish thought the idea impossible — foolhardy and dangerous, certainly, but not impossible. Both aviators stressed that flying from Scotland to Australia in a light aircraft was achievable, but to succeed would take a great deal of preparation and forethought.

For George, this acknowledgement was the deciding factor.

The next significant decision to be made concerned me and my involvement. If I agreed to accompany him, then I would take a course in navigation and act as number two crew member. If I decided not to participate, George would respect my decision and we would continue with our wedding plans. George would travel solo to Australia and, when he reached his destination, I would join him, travelling by more conventional means. In 1968, more conventional meant a six-week sea journey by passenger cruise-liner for a fare of £10, now widely known as ten pound poms.

—

Being young and in love, the decision wasn't too difficult. I was absolutely certain that I would not be able to live with myself if my best friend and true love lost his life, or worse, vanished without a trace. At that age, I still had the belief that I was somehow invincible and philosophised that if we were together everything would be 'all right'. So, despite my parents' distress, I agreed to join him in the flight and act as navigator crew member number two.

—

Persuading, or should I say convincing, our parents that such a journey was achievable was not easy. My father said outright that it could not be done in such a small craft; whereupon George, using an atlas and details of our intended route, confidently and patiently explained how it could be done. They would not be convinced. However, when our respective families realised that nothing would make us see sense, they uncompromisingly gave us all their support.

All the staff and most of the members of the Edinburgh Aero Club supported and encouraged our ambitious adventure. Ian taught me how to calculate a flight path from a weather report using only a simple navigator's slide rule and a ruler. Wing Commander Jock Dalgleish supplied us with redundant topographical defence force maps. They also provided expert advice in planning a route that would minimise the number of water crossings. Single-engine aircraft flying long distances over water is regarded as high risk and certainly not recommended.

—

On 7 March, 1968, George made his first solo flight in a single-engine Cessna aircraft. We married on 5 April that year and on 22 April George graduated as a fully qualified private pilot with a grand total of forty-four hours and fifty minutes flying experience.

Wing Commander Dalgleish mentored the purchase of a Beagle Terrier aircraft, with the British call sign Golf Alpha Sierra Charlie Golf or GASCG, thereafter affectionately called 'Charlie Golf'. Incidentally, Charlie Golf was purchased on our wedding day.

Watching George learn to fly Charlie Golf was both entertaining and nerve-wracking.

One afternoon, my brother-in-law and I were watching George bring Charlie Golf down onto the runway outside the Edinburgh Aero Club. It so happened that another trainee pilot was practising the same manoeuvres in an identical aircraft at the same time. These manoeuvres are aptly called circuits and bumps.

On touch down, George didn't quite get Charlie Golf's three

wheels onto the runway simultaneously, with the result the aircraft bounced for several hundred yards, each time hitting the tarmac with a heavy thud, whereupon the tail started to swing from side to side. Once this happens, the pilot has virtually lost control and all one can do is pray. From the aero club we watched aghast as Charlie Golf turned a full circle, slewed sideways and mounted the grass verge before coming to a halt. Moments later, the second pilot hit the tarmac hard, bounced several times, turned a full circle and slewed sideways then came to a halt on the opposite grass verge.

Although unhurt, both pilots were shaken. That whole scenario looked like a well-rehearsed circus act and was much talked about in the clubhouse for many weeks later.

Jock and Ian inspired us, encouraged us to believe in ourselves and our abilities, and gave us the confidence to turn a blind eye to the many doubting members of the Aero Club who predicted that we wouldn't even get as far as the English Channel. We would surely come a cropper on the first day somewhere over England!

Sadly, one of those very doubters lost his own life in a tragic light aircraft accident in Scotland while we were preparing for our journey.

Other sceptics included the oil companies and aircraft manufacturers we had approached for sponsorship. They all shook their heads in amusement declaring that such a trip was foolhardy and could not be done by two such rank amateurs. The British Immigration Department (we had already been granted permanent resident visas for Australia) also refused to ship our heavy luggage out to Australia for £10, even though we were saving them the expense of our own travel.

We tried many avenues, but it soon became clear that no-one was prepared to sponsor our trip and we would have to meet all our own expenses. We had estimated our expenses to be somewhere in the region of £3,500, virtually all our life savings in 1968.

Once the necessary flight clearances had come through and the last minute shopping and packing was done, we set the date for departure. I recall phoning my mother to tell her we would be leaving the following Wednesday. To my surprise her response was 'Oh! So you're definitely going then?' Clearly, close family was still finding it difficult to accept that we were determined to embark on this mad adventure.

So on 19 June 1968, in a single-engine aircraft with no navigation aids except a compass and equipped only for visual flight, we departed Edinburgh Turnhouse Aerodrome and took to the skies on the first leg of our journey to Australia.

Planning their route . . . Kathleen and George, helped by Wing Commander Dalgleish

Planning the route

George swinging the propeller ready to taxi while family anxiously watch on

A final farewell

Chapter 2

England

Learning the ropes

Wednesday 19 June 1968
Edinburgh — Brough, England
Time of departure: 07.37 GMT Flying time: 4hrs
Flying conditions: Low cloud, thunderstorms and sea mist.
Wind direction and velocity: 260°/15knots.

As George's private pilot's licence was for visual flight only, the low cloud and possible storms meant that we were unable to stick to our original flight plan overland to Southend. Instead, we were forced to fly at an altitude somewhere between 500 and 2500ft down the east coast of Scotland and England. Charlie Golf had a flying time of no more than four-and-a-half hours, depending on weather conditions and wind strength and, as such, the deviation along the coastline meant we were forced to refuel at Brough on the east coast of England.

—

Brough — Southend, England
Time of departure: 14.34 GMT Flying time: 2hrs 26mins
Flying conditions: Low cloud and sea mist. Wind direction and velocity: 260°/15knots.

As we tracked the cliffs along the coastline south of Brough, much to our horror a fighter jet suddenly appeared out of the cloud on our starboard side. The jet appeared to have come from a disused airfield and was travelling at the same altitude as Charlie Golf. It was so close we could see the pilot. We had no prior warning of RAF (Royal Air Force) activity in the area and although we were flying visual flight and had spotted the jet travel across in front of us, our real concern was that the pilot's mates may be following behind. The remainder of the flight from Brough to Southend was spent keenly searching the skies to avoid a mid-air collision should other aircraft be within close proximity.

Brough to Southend added a further two hours and twenty minutes onto the estimated four-hour flight from Scotland and we finally arrived over Southend at 17.00 local time. Much to our disappointment, the inclement weather meant that we had to ask Southend air traffic control for a QDM, an aviation term for home tracing to a station. When a pilot asks for a QDM, the air traffic controller advises the pilot of the correct compass heading to set that would give the most direct and safest flight path to the airport.

At the end of every flight it was normal procedure on arriving at an airport to report to Air Traffic Control to debrief, check in with customs and immigration and advise the authorities of the pilot's intentions regarding length of stay, departure time and next destination. The pilot would also be given detailed information about the weather and flying conditions for the next few days. This procedure enabled us to plan our ongoing schedule with some degree of confidence.

That first night away from home was spent in a moderately cheap, private hotel. Given our lack of sponsorship and limited financial resources, low cost accommodation and meagre living expenses was a necessity.

Prior to leaving our home city of Glasgow, we received a reasonable amount of local media coverage through various newspapers. In the main, the reports were factual and positive, with a tendency to dwell on the, "newly married", "honeymoon" and other perceived romantic aspects of the story. One reporter couldn't pass up the opportunity to link our story with the famous Wright brothers. The most amusing of all was an article printed in the newspapers the morning following our wedding the previous day: "All set to a flying start to married life, George Wright and his wife Kathleen ..." While the reporter managed to get the basic information correct, the accompanying photograph was not that of George and Kathleen Wright, but of another couple who just happened to be married in the same church earlier on the same Friday afternoon — so it was no great surprise when we arrived at the hotel in Southend to receive a telephone call from yet another reporter requesting an interview.

To give ourselves time to recover from the emotional side of leaving family and friends behind, we decided to spend two nights in Southend before venturing across the English Channel. What better way to relax than to go to the pub for a few drinks followed by a greasy, English, fish supper wrapped in newspaper.

You might think that George and I, being young people of the 1960s, would be dabbling in the psychedelic drug scene. Not so. Neither of us experimented with drugs, although many of our acquaintances did. George was a heavy smoker. I was not. Our vice of choice was alcohol. In the '60s, there was no stigma attached to drinking alcohol and so we partied hard — very hard — on light ale or heavy beer and whisky for the guys; and lager, vodka and orange, or rum and Coke for the girls. Our social life revolved around the pub scene, drinking parties, or the local jazz club. Alcohol was a major part of our social life and was a determining factor in how and where we spent our free time.

That being said, it was quite normal for George and I to

head to the pub and consume a few drinks before our evening meal, especially if we had nothing significant planned for the following day.

—

Thursday 20 June
Southend, England

After a 9.00am breakfast George and I returned to Southend airport to check on Charlie Golf and to file a flight plan for the following day. After wandering round Southend in the rain, we returned to the hotel to discover that the media wanted photographs of George and I alongside Charlie Golf. We were duly whisked back to the airport where we posed for the photographer alongside our small, single-engine aircraft in the wind and rain. The ensuing newspaper article read:

Said George, "My hobby is flying and I bought the plane six months ago after getting my licence. We will sell it when we reach Australia so we have money to set ourselves up." The aircraft is equipped with a radio and the couple have only a compass and map to show them the way. Kathleen will be doing the map reading and "George will have to fly low enough for me to get our bearings," she said, just before the silver and white plane soared into the blue over Southend.

Chapter 3

France

Inexperience shows and reality sets in

Friday 21 June 1968
Southend — Calais, France
Time of departure: 11.11 GMT   Flying time: 1hr 57mins
Flying conditions: Thunderstorms sleet and rain. Wind direction and velocity: 260°/20knots

That morning, the weather forecast for flying across the channel was abysmal. The prediction was for thunderstorms, sleet and rain. The meteorological (Met) forecasters advised that they expected the low cloud to eventually lift to an acceptable altitude that would enable visual flight. For this reason we hung around Southend Airport. At 11.00am, having cleared customs and with a flight plan direct to Dijon duly filed and acknowledged, we eventually took off into what was to be short-lived clear skies.

Approximately ten minutes after take-off, we encountered reasonably severe thunderstorm activity. To avoid the hazard, we had to fly low over the water and deviate from our intended flight path. We eventually sighted land on the French side of the channel. However, we were unable to make radio contact with the Paris controllers. We also had no alternative frequencies to access other than the emergency frequency.

In those flying conditions, it was extremely difficult to identify land marks and locate our exact position. To avoid exacerbating our plight, and with no radio contact, George decided to land at the nearest available airfield. Unfortunately, this turned out to be the Belgian military airfield of Coxyde. As the navigator, this was an extremely embarrassing start to an epic journey that was supposed to take us across continents.

Thankfully, the military officials were extremely gracious and sympathetic towards our plight and, with the newly acquired knowledge of our exact location and a working radio frequency, we were able to take off and continue an uneventful flight to Calais. We cleared customs inward at Calais and checked the Meteorological Office (Met) report for our onward flight to Dijon. Once again, the forecast predicted possible thunderstorms, low cloud and poor visibility. As such, we decided to call it quits for the day and spend the night in Calais.

We ate French omelette for our evening meal at Calais Airport and at about 8.00pm George asked the barman to recommend overnight accommodation that was reasonably cheap. My diary for that day reads:

Here I sit in a tiny cubicle that contains 1 double bed, 1 sink and 1 chair. The walls are made of paper and there are 3 glass vents above a wooden planking door. A sign hanging on the door reads Chambre 7-9 francs. The noises emanating from the accommodation's bar are distinctly audible and will surely keep us awake all night.

That was cheap accommodation, but after such a disastrous day's flying, we slept well.

Saturday 22 June

Calais – Dijon Longvic, France

Time of departure: 11.41 GMT   Flying time: 3hrs 09mins

Flying conditions: Drizzle and mist followed by fine sunshine.

Wind direction and velocity: 240°/25knots.

We awoke on Saturday morning to a very cold, cloudy and drizzly day. Despite this, we headed out to Calais Airport to see what the Met men had to say about our chances of flying. We were told that the inclement weather was local and that once we cleared Calais the cloud base would lift. We decided the risks were minimal and so took off for Dijon. After our flying experiences of the last three days, the flight to Dijon was idyllic and incident free, that is, apart from having great difficulty deciphering what the French air traffic controller was saying. The weather forecast turned out to be accurate and we flew south at 3000ft over the lush green fields of France. Our time of arrival at Dijon Longvic was 2.50pm, giving us a ground speed of 70mph.

—

Dijon Longvic — Marseille, France

Time of departure: 16.17 GMT Flying time: 4hrs 05mins
Flying conditions: Clear skies, good visibility. Wind direction and velocity: 200°/10knots

On arrival at Dijon, a French military base, we discovered there were no additional facilities available to us other than refuelling Charlie Golf. After considering the excellent weather conditions and the distance to Marseille from Dijon (231nautical miles), we decided to continue on to Marseille. We reasoned we had ample flying time to reach our destination before dusk at 19.30. Our flight south that late afternoon gave us magnificent breathtaking views of the French Alps. Although we were constantly alert and vigilant with our flying regime, we felt we could allow ourselves to relax and enjoy the splendour around us, that is, until our estimated land speed according to our topographical maps seemed to be much slower than we had first calculated.

We determined that the only possible reason for this had to

be a substantial difference between the estimated wind velocity and direction as provided by the Dijon forecasters and the actual conditions we were experiencing. This meant, of course, that our estimated time of arrival into Marseille would be much later than first calculated. We reasoned that at least we would have enough fuel to get us to the airport. George reduced our altitude in an attempt to avoid the strong head wind, but it made little difference to our land speed. Apart from this, the skies remained absolutely clear and we had excellent visual flight conditions.

As we turned Charlie Golf towards the Mediterranean coast, we could see the coastal villages and the city of Marseille quite clearly in the distance. As per usual procedure, George transferred radio frequency and reported in to Marseille air traffic control, who would have been expecting us as per the flight we filed in Dijon. When Marseille's controllers radioed back, it was obvious they were not at all happy about the discrepancy in our estimated time of arrival. George tried to explain that we were flying a light aircraft and experiencing forceful headwinds that were considerably inhibiting our speed. We gave an assurance that we had the airport and the main runway in sight and would be in a position to carry out a 'straight in' approach without jeopardising safety. By the time we started landing preparations, the controllers had switched on the main runway lights for us. The evening dusk was ablaze with the power of the lights.

By this time we were both frazzled and on edge. Despite this, George perfected the landing with aplomb and we were relieved to be on *terra firma*. The log shows that the flight that should have taken about two and three-quarter hours actually took four hours and five minutes. As we taxied towards the designated parking bay, the voice over the radio announced, 'Would the pilot of Golf Alpha Sierra Charlie Golf please report to the control tower immediately.' We knew we were in for a hard time. Despite our explanations, George was given a severe dressing down for conducting visual flight after dusk without instruments. Had it not been for the intervention of one particular officer, the matter would have been reported to the British air authorities.

We were so exhausted and cranky after the events of the past few days that we adopted an attitude of *so what, we don't intend to go back anyway*. Of course we did not voice this opinion openly, but it was to be the first of many during our four-month journey.

It was 10.30 in the evening by the time we cleared the officialdom at the airport and, as we hadn't eaten since 8.00am, we decided to dine at the airport before heading into the city. It was then we noticed the magnificent trappings of Marseille International Airport. We felt uncomfortably grubby and decidedly out of place as we made our way through the marble halls and staircases, chandeliers, neon lights and expensive retail outlets.

Once in the city, and because it was such a balmy evening, we went for a stroll round the harbour crammed with yachts and cruisers of all shapes and sizes. The diary jottings for that long exhausting day notes that we eventually hit the sack at 2.00am.

—

Sunday 23 June
Marseille, France

We woke on Sunday morning to dark, cloudy skies. About the time we were contemplating returning to the airport for a more defined Met report, the heavens opened and down came the rain. As we were browsing the Marseille markets, I felt my mood changing and before long I was struggling with very deep depression. I am sure it was the after-effects of the intensity, stress and stuff-ups of the previous few days as well as a hefty dose of homesickness. I recall suddenly being faced with the possibility that I may perish on this mad escapade and would never see loved ones again. I was full of doubt and uncertainty about what we hoped to achieve. I was scared.

To make matters worse, we got lost in the back streets of Marseille trying to find our way back to the hotel. Once at the hotel, we shook off the wet gear and, after a raging argument, ventured out once more to find a local wine bar where we could order lunch and drinks. After several martinis, my depression worsened and I ended up a sobbing mess, so much so that George had to put me to bed. I recovered after a sound sleep and in the early evening we once again took in the sights, sounds and smells of the French Mediterranean port. There must have been an election in progress as we came upon what seemed be a victory march of a political nature. French flags and red flags were abundant and the demonstrators appeared to be in a celebratory mood.

Chapter 4

Corsica and Sardinia

Embarrassing take-off and Mediterranean delights

Monday 24 June 1968
Marseille – Ajaccio, Corsica (via Nice)
Time of departure: 11.03 GMT   Flying time: 2hrs 48mins
Flying conditions: Strong wind gusts, clear visibility, sea haze. Wind direction and velocity: 320°/40knots.

That morning the weather was on our side. We woke at 7.00am to clear blue skies, so we packed our gear and made our way back to Marseille International Airport. As it was mid-morning by the time we fuelled up Charlie Golf, filed a flight plan for the next stage and cleared customs, the airport was busy with air traffic and travellers. As we taxied along the approach to our designated take-off runway, it became clear that the strong winds of two days before had not abated. Single-engine aircraft with overhead wings and tail wheel have a tendency to flip over in a strong crosswind. In the crosswind gusting at 40 knots, Charlie Golf shook, then tilted dangerously until the starboard wing was almost scraping the tarmac. In a bid to avoid total disaster, George yelled out, 'Quick, get the f*** out there and hang onto that b****y wing strut before we tip over.' In blind panic, I leaped out of the moving aircraft and jumped up to grab the struts of the port wing as it swung up and down. George continued to slowly taxi Charlie Golf down the long taxiway with me swinging and hanging on to those struts for dear life. At times my feet were lifted 2ft off the ground. Three buttons were ripped off my shirt in the melee. Thankfully, the strategy worked and Charlie Golf was still upright when we reached the take-off runway. However, just as George swung Charlie Golf round to line up for take-off, we were hit by another strong gust of wind. Charlie Golf's tail swung round too far and sheared off one of the lights at the side of the taxiway. I recall George again yelling at the top of his voice, 'For God's sake, get the f*** back in. No way are we stopping or we'll never get away from this god-forsaken airport.'

I quickly dropped to the ground and furtively scrambled back into the moving cockpit as the aircraft continued to roll forward.

Assuring air traffic control that nothing was amiss (we omitted to mention the broken light), we lined up and proceeded with a rolling take-off. However, our troubles were not over. Because of the excessively strong head winds, it took Charlie Golf about 20 minutes to clear the main runway and by the time we did we were flying at an altitude of 2,500ft. It was like going up in an elevator while creeping forward.

We decided we would not be welcomed back to Marseille International Airport, but thought we must have been a great source of amusement for the travellers standing out on the airport verandas.

Local regulations determined we must overfly Nice on our way to Corsica. As we turned on course towards Nice, the winds were still gusting between 25 and 45 knots. Under those conditions Charlie Golf would suddenly drop 500ft in altitude when in fact it should have been climbing. The experience gave us a few anxious moments over the mountainous terrain. The log indicates that on some sections over the mountains, we were flying at 8,000ft.

Once we cleared the coast, the crossing over the sea to Ajaccio was pleasant and uneventful and we arrived at the time estimated on our flight plan. The exceptionally well maintained flying club at Ajaccio was a welcome relief after the hair-raising events of the morning and so we were thankful for a bite to eat and the ability to freshen up before we embarked on the short second stage of the day.

—

Ajaccio — Alghero, Sardinia

Time of departure: 16.25 GMT Flying time: 1hr.03mins
Flying conditions: Light wind gusts, clear visibility. Wind direction and velocity: 320°/15knots.

After clearing customs outbound from Ajaccio, our journey to Alghero was thankfully pleasant and uneventful, although we did have some difficulty locating the airfield. Once on the ground, we were met by Italian custom officials and allowed to house Charlie Golf under cover in a hanger. The officials at Alghero were exceptionally considerate and helpful. They quickly dealt with the necessary paperwork and organised a taxi to take us into Alghero. We specifically asked the taxi driver to take us to a cheap hotel, but where did we end up — at the Grand Hotel with marble staircases, terrazzo flooring, and a room with a balcony, en-suite bathroom with hot and cold showers ... and ... single beds. Although we knew it would cost a fortune, we reasoned we deserved to spoil ourselves and enjoy a little of luxury. Feeling relaxed, we used the opportunity to dress for dinner. George put on the suit he bought specially for the trip: a cream, light-weight, tailored suit specially made for travellers on the move. He looked great ... very handsome. By the time we retired at midnight, we both agreed Alghero was a delightful place and the Italians were better cooks and much easier to get along with than the French.

—

Tuesday 25 June

Alghero – Cagliari, Sardinia

Time of departure: 10.58 GMT Flying time: 1hr 46mins
Flying conditions: Clear skies, hot, turbulence over mountains. Wind direction and velocity: n/a.

We rose late on Tuesday — too late for breakfast — so we had to make do with a coffee to start the day. As Cagliari was only a short distance away and the weather appeared to be favourable, we decided to push on with our travels. When we got to the airport, we were told that we would have to wait over two hours for the avgas bowser, so we took off for Cagliari without refuelling Charlie Golf. We could not plan a route direct to Cagliari because the regulations forbid flying over danger zones. However, the deviation did not add much mileage to the trip and the journey from one island to the other was pleasant and uneventful.

On reaching Cagliari, our plan was to stay put for a few days of rest and relaxation before proceeding to North Africa, but when we arrived we were disappointed to find that Cagliari was a large town and not the beachside resort we had hoped for. On arrival, the authorities were very friendly. The ground engineers in particular were extremely curious and fascinated with Charlie Golf.

After we cleared the airport, we had great difficulty communicating with the taxi driver. Following several rather frustrating misunderstandings, we eventually got the driver to take us to a hotel by the beach. Once settled into the hotel, we enjoyed a much needed swim in the warm Mediterranean Sea and a chance to lie on the beach and soak up the sun. When it was time to eat, we discovered there were no restaurant amenities in or near the hotel and we were told we would have to take a bus back into Cagliari. Our frustration was further fuelled when George realised he had almost no Italian *lira* left and the hotel receptionist refused to cash a cheque. Feeling very disgruntled, we found some local shops and, with the few notes and coins we had left, we managed to buy a BBQ chicken, bread and some cheese. We took it all back to the hotel and ate in our room.

We had been advised that Tunisia, our next destination, required twenty-four hours' notice before we could land at their airport. This supported our initial decision to stop over for a day or two and catch up with some chores.

The most immediate chore, of course, was washing clothes. Apart from the necessary underwear and socks, my wardrobe consisted of: one pair of lightweight denim jeans; two cotton, button-through shirts; one pair of stretch, fitting trousers; one short-sleeved top; one lightweight parka; one short-sleeved, mid-length, cotton dress; one very short, stretch-lurex dress for special occasions; one polyester skirt; one pair of dress shoes and one pair sneakers. George had two pair of jeans; a couple of shirts; a light-weight dress suit; dress shirt; one tie; underwear; socks; and a lightweight, quilted jacket.

I had to manage the laundry whenever we had spare time and generally it was done in the hotel bathroom sink using toilet soap to wash and any furniture that was handy for hanging clothes out to dry. If it wasn't dry by the time we had to leave, it went into the suitcase in a plastic bag. As best we could, we tried to maintain our personal hygiene and keep our clothes clean and respectable.

The second task, when we had time, was keeping our

relatives in Scotland informed of our progress. This was vital as we knew they would be worried if they didn't hear from us. In 1968, of course, there were no mobile telephones, no internet, Facebook or email. Landline wasn't a viable option as we did not know the overseas telephone codes and trying to conduct long distance conversations with the annoying delay echo was too daunting. As such, whenever possible, we bought local picture postcards, wrote a few cursory but informative lines on the back, then sent them alternately to each side of the family. If my parents got a card from Marseille, George's family would get the next one from Corsica. When the families received their postcards, they circulated the latest news to keep everyone informed of our progress and adventures.

The most important task of all was plotting our route for the next day's flight. I did this every evening before retiring and George would check my calculations before filing a flight plan the following day. To plot the route, I used an everyday ruler and drew a straight line that joined the airport of departure to the airport of our intended destination. Positioning the compass across the line and lining up due north gave me the actual compass direction. I then factored in the wind direction and velocity and this gave me the actual compass heading to set. Once in the air, George maintained the compass heading with visual flight while I navigated and confirmed our actual flying position with the topographical map and the terrain below.

The last task, of course, was to accurately document in my diary the most salient and memorable aspects of that day's experiences.

That hot stuffy night in Cagliari was no different from many others. I wrote postcards, washed clothes, brought the diary up to date and made initial preparations for our flight to Tunisia.

—

Wednesday 26 June
Cagliari, Sardinia

This morning we rose early as we had to return to the airport to file our flight plan, giving Tunisia the required twenty-four hours' notice. The first stop was finding the post office to send cards and the bank to exchange money. The post office was easy to find. However, we got lost trying to locate a bank. After walking for ages, we eventually climbed aboard a bus that took us straight there.

With money in our pockets once again, we wandered through the town until we found a comfortable bar where we could quench our thirst with a cool beer. The people in the bar were exceptionally friendly and over a few beers wanted to know all about us, where we were from, and where we were going. We befriended a student and he accompanied us in the taxi back to the airport. He was most intrigued with the process of filing a flight plan. We all returned to the bar and had a few more Sardinian beers before George and I wandered off to find somewhere to eat lunch.

Once again we got friendly with the locals and ended up drinking beer and eating whole fish fried and huge sardines with lashings of lemon juice — very delicious. However, when one of the older men picked the eyes out of his fish and popped them in his mouth then crunched his teeth into the fish's head, I decided it was time to go for a swim and sunbake on the beach. George continued to drink for a while, and then before he left for a swim he arranged to meet one of the locals, who happened to be a police officer, in the hotel bar at 8.00pm. The diary notes indicate that we went back to the bar for more drinks, then ate an evening meal of spaghetti and mussels before retiring at midnight somewhat worse for wear.

That night was pure hell. I recalled earlier in the evening sitting on the bed enjoying the sea breeze with the veranda doors wide open. As I wrote up the diary, I noticed lots of black insects flying round me. They were emanating a high pitched buzzing sound and, when swatted and squashed, they left a splotch of red blood on the skin or the bed cover. This was to be my first encounter with dreaded mosquitoes and, of course, I did not know the damage they could do if you happened to be allergic to them, as I was. That night those parts of my anatomy that had been exposed to the elements while I sat on the bed were covered in unbearably itchy, large, red bites. The itching drove me almost crazy and I don't think I got more than ten minutes shut-eye the whole night. To add to my discomfort, it was unbearably hot and because of the mosquitoes we were unable to sleep with the veranda doors open for relief.

Chapter 5

Tunisia

Africa; a whole new world with sensory overload

Thursday 27 June 1968
Cagliari — Tunis, Tunisia
Time of departure: 8.10 GMT   Flying time: 1hr 59mins
Flying conditions: Hot, clear skies, haze on horizon. Wind direction and velocity: 330°/10knots.

Despite the bad night, or maybe because of it, I rose at dawn. The two of us quickly dressed, got our gear together, then made our way to the airport. We were excited about this stage of our travels. George and I had spent a couple of holidays in the past travelling through France, Italy and Spain, so our experiences with the French and Italians in Europe were not altogether new. Africa, however, was. It seemed that this was the real beginning of our adventure into the unknown. We both knew deep inside that there would be no turning back once we crossed the Mediterranean. So after completing the necessary administration, we took off for Tunis with light-hearted anticipation. This was also our first flight over water and out of sight of land. I can't believe that I was not the least bit nervous.

Because we were flying over water, my job as navigator was not required as long as we flew to the correct compass settings as per the flight plan. This enabled me to take a spell with the controls for the first time since we left Edinburgh — an indication of how relaxed and confident we were feeling.

The sea haze did not inhibit our visual flight and our first sight of the African coast was truly awesome. I recall the magnificent glow of the vivid red-orange horizon against the cool green-blue of the Mediterranean Sea — quite splendid and breathtaking.

So far on our travels we had not taken many photographs or used the movie camera. We found that flying and navigating over unknown terrain was extremely demanding and the opportunity to take pictures did not present itself very often. However, this stage of our journey was different and we managed to record the magnificent vista unfolding before us on the movie camera.

Tunis airport came into view right on time and George made an excellent "straight-in" approach with a perfect landing. We were getting used to the idea that every time we entered or departed a country the customs and immigration procedures were demanding and lengthy. For the first time we were ordered to declare all our monies. Even though we had another stop in Tunisia, we reported to the control tower and advised them of our intention to travel to Tripoli in Libya. Once again the authorities were extremely friendly and helpful. The universal language of air traffic is English, but we discovered the language spoken by Tunisians is French.

Using a tourist brochure, we picked out a rather splendid hotel in the city of Tunis. After settling in, we wandered the streets taking in the sights and smells of the city. We noticed that the older women wore what looked like white flowing robes that also came up over their heads and covered their faces. Most of the men wore tiny, red, skull caps on the back of their heads.

We ate a delicious lunch of pasta bought in a street side café and continued our walk. By this time, the streets and alleyways were coming alive as we soaked up the atmosphere of the shops and stalls of the bazaars. We were in awe of the magnificent, dazzling white, old buildings with turrets painted with many bright contrasting colours, truly a splendid sight especially with the added glow of the street lights. In direct contrast, we were confronted with our first experience of maimed and disfigured street beggars using trolleys with wheels to propel themselves along the dusty alleyways. We realised that, as foreign tourists, we were the beggars' obvious targets. We were spellbound and our senses were in overload by the time we returned to the hotel. Everything was so new and there was so much more we wanted to see and experience.

—

Friday 28 June
Tunis, Tunisia

We woke to another day of splendid, hot, sunny weather and decided to wear bathers under our shirts and jeans. After a breakfast of chicken and ham sandwiches, beer and Coke, we ventured out into the streets once more to find a post office to send off the cards purchased and written the night before. We then walked to the train station in the main street and bought two return tickets to the beach suburb of Carthage-Aimilcar. The train was ancient with rickety carriages and wooden bench seats. As we trundled along, we hung out of the windows to keep cool just like the locals were doing. We were amazed at the opulence of some buildings as the train passed through what was obviously a wealthy quarter of the city. The sandy beach and blue sea did not disappoint. We lazed, swam and sun-baked for a couple of hours and then when George felt he'd had enough sun, we had more chicken sandwiches and beers in a very high-priced hotel across the road from the beach.

Feeling very relaxed and happy but exhausted, we made our way back up the hill to the station to catch a train back into Tunis. By the time we got back to the hotel it was quite apparent that George had had far too much sun and was badly burned on his arms, back, face and neck. The only remedy we had available was cold cream, so we lavishly plastered it on his burns, hoping it would give him some relief. George was so uncomfortable, he went to bed and had a late afternoon sleep. He was feeling much better when he woke, but we still didn't venture far from the hotel for our evening meal.

—

Saturday 29 June
Tunis – Djerba, Tunisia

Time of departure: 05.25 GMT Flying time: 2hrs 52mins
Flying conditions: Extremely poor visibility due to haze. Wind direction and velocity: 060°/20knots.

In extreme hot weather, Charlie Golf does not get the necessary airlift to become airborne or to reach the required altitude. For this reason, it was safer for us to take off and fly in the coolest part of the day. This was why we were out of bed at 4.00am and at the airport chatting with air traffic controllers by 5.00.

After we cleared Tunis air space, we were unable to pick up the radio frequency for Djerba as advised by Tunis air traffic control. Our plight progressively worsened as the visibility was so bad due to the thick, low haze. I had trouble navigating and we almost missed the island altogether, despite the fact we were following the coastline.

On sighting the airfield, we were still unable to make radio contact. As if things couldn't be worse, we were also unable to locate a windsock that would give us an accurate wind direction for a safe landing. Given we had to refuel, we had no alternative but to land. George followed the accepted international procedure for such circumstances and circled the Djerba control tower three times at three different altitudes. No response was forthcoming in the way of flag signals and we received no acknowledgement that the controllers were aware of our presence. As such, George proceeded to put Charlie Golf down on the runway without permission. We both found this whole experience very harrowing and nerve-wracking. To add to our distress, just as Charlie Golf's wheels touched the tarmac, we got caught in a wind gust and the aircraft did a 360° ground loop. Not only was this scary, but also extremely embarrassing. Fortunately, George was aware of Charlie Golf's tendency to do this and was able to quickly bring the aircraft back under control.

Considering the circumstances, the authorities at Djerba were relatively affable. However, we were quite rattled and felt that the air traffic controllers were partly to blame for our dilemmas.

Chapter 6

Libya

Radio troubles and bad landings

Saturday 29 June 1968
Djerba — Tripoli, Libya
Time of departure: 10.56 GMT Flying time: 1hr 44mins
Flying conditions: Dust, poor visibility with haze. Wind direction & velocity: 360°/20knots.

After a considerable delay in the stifling heat, we took off for Tripoli, but even this short leg of the journey was riddled with misadventure and could have ended in disaster.

We had no problems with take-off and, as the visibility still hadn't improved, we followed the coastline at 3,000ft. We were both edgy and in bad humour. Not a good combination when working together in a limited space and extremely hot weather. We both had short fuses. The city of Tripoli appeared in the distance within the predicted time frame. However, we very quickly realised that once more something was amiss with the radio frequency provided by Djerba and air traffic control. Setting our course on the topographical map, I had routed our flight to Tripoli Wheelus airfield. Unfortunately, unknown to us, Tripoli Wheelus was a military airfield. The radio frequency provided by Djerba was for Tripoli Idris, the international airport.

Therefore, it was no wonder we were totally confused. After circling Wheelus several times, I suddenly realised that we had radio contact with the airport fifteen miles south of our current position — that is, Tripoli Idris. As if things couldn't get worse, the wind was extremely turbulent at altitudes lower than 1,000ft and George had to work hard to bring Charlie Golf down with minimum bounce from the upward draughts. As the wheels touched the runway, Charlie Golf repeated the performance of earlier in the day and proceeded to swing into another very hairy 360° ground loop with the wind tipping the wings almost to the tarmac. My heart was in my mouth, but George was able to keep control of Charlie Golf and no damage was done.

Custom and immigration officials took forever to process our papers and, to our alarm, they insisted on keeping our passports and the pilot's log book. We were told we would have them returned on departure. With Charlie Golf refuelled, we made our way up to the control tower to apologise for our navigation blunder. Much to our amazement, and delight, the air traffic controllers were British. They appeared to accept our embarrassing explanations and informed us that, in fact, we should not have been allowed to land in Libya at all as we did not have a civil aviation permit. Unlike the large commercial airlines, single-engine private aircraft travellers such as ourselves had little access to this level of information and the officials in Tunisia had failed to advise us of the need for a permit.

Unfortunately, this lack of information and communication between civil aviation and immigration authorities across borders was to be a very worrying trend throughout our entire journey.

Our fellow citizens in Tripoli air traffic control also informed us that we would be unable to refuel at Marble Arch on our way to Benghazi. However, after some anxious discussions over the topographical maps, they helped us find an alternative airfield within acceptable range.

Their friendship did not end there. One air traffic controller named Whin Watkins offered to put us up for the night as, in his words, 'the prices of hotels in this part of the world are extortionately high'. We arranged to meet at the airport bus terminal at the conclusion of his shift. George and I spent the next hour or so in the airport bar and befriended yet another British compatriot. After such a horrific day's flying, we found Whin's flat to be very comfortable and most welcoming. Whin prepared juicy steaks for dinner and we chatted over glasses of wine for quite some time before turning in at midnight. Whin suggested we spend the next day in Tripoli before resuming our travels and we wholeheartedly agreed.

Many times that day I asked myself what I had got myself into and came to the conclusion it couldn't get much worse. I was very wrong.

—

Sunday 30 June
Tripoli, Libya

Apart from a disturbing rumpus caused by one of Whin's friends returning from a party sometime in the middle of the night, George and I slept soundly 'til 11.30am. We breakfasted on strong, black coffee and Whin made an appearance just as we finished our chores. We talked 'til 3.00pm, whereupon our host suggested we take a walk through the city to visit the old bazaar and the king's palace. You would think after all this time we would be experts at getting ourselves around unfamiliar cities. Not so. We got lost again, but eventually did manage to find the king's palace and the old bazaar. After the splendour of Tunis, we found Tripoli to be a little disappointing. On our way back to Whin's flat, we stocked up on groceries, beer and cigarettes.

Whin had cooked a splendid spaghetti bolognaise dinner for us and invited his neighbours to join us. The only problem was, by the time we all got together, Whin was well and truly "in his cups". However, I was able to serve the meal for the assembled company. Whin's neighbours, an Englishman who worked with Whin in air traffic control, his Austrian wife and their three children, made good company. We all enjoyed a sociable evening and only called a halt when we realised how well and truly drunk our host had become.

—

Monday 1 July

Tripoli — Ras Lanuf, Libya

Time of departure: 08.18 GMT Flying time: 4hrs.06mins
Flying conditions: Hot, excessive sand haze, poor visibility.
Wind direction and velocity: 330°/10knots.

George and I, slightly worse for wear, rose at 7.00am to find Whin still sleeping on the chair in which we had left him the night before. We did leave a "thank you" note for when he surfaced. Fortunately, his friend Peter offered to take us to the airport in his car as other airport staff may not have appreciated us using their staff bus.

We collected our passports and log book, refuelled Charlie Golf, then filed a flight plan for Ras Lanuf, the alternative airstrip to Marble Arch.

The four-plus hours' flight along the coast to Ras Lanuf was exceptionally hot and boring. Once again, the visibility was limited by the thick haze caused by sand rising up from the flat, orange desert. Not much to do and too much time to ponder the enormity of what we had taken on.

The heat seemed more intense at Ras Lanuf Mobil Airfield. Apart from fuel for Charlie Golf, there were no other amenities available where we could eat and freshen up. We decided the best plan would be to press on to Benghazi.

—

Ras Lanuf – Benghazi, Libya

Time of departure: 13.16 GMT Flying time: 2hrs 19mins
Flying conditions: Hot, humid, sand haze, poor visibility. Wind direction and velocity: 330°/10knots.

By this time we were hot, tired, hungry and extremely irritable. George and I were just not used to such extreme heat and we probably weren't drinking enough water. This was certainly not the best circumstances for light-aircraft flying.

After another disagreement relating to my navigation techniques, or lack thereof, we eventually sighted Benghazi airport and managed to approach and land without any more mishaps. It was 10.00pm by the time we cleared customs and immigration, refuelled Charlie Golf and arranged our onward flight to Egypt. Once ensconced in a high-priced hotel in the heart of Benghazi, we freshened up, had a few drinks at the hotel bar and then paid a fantastic amount of money for a very ordinary meal. After being hurriedly ushered out of the café, we returned to the hotel bar for more drinks then crashed into bed, very tired and travel-weary.

—

Tuesday 2 July

Benghazi – El Adem, Libya

Time of departure: 08.46 GMT Flying time: 3hrs.24mins
Flying conditions: Low level turbulence, down draught over high terrain. Wind direction and velocity: n/a.

We must have rested reasonably well, as the diary indicates we checked in at Benghazi airport at 7.30. Much to our relief, we were advised that we had been granted clearance to fly from Libya into Egypt, so we took off in a much better frame of mind than that of the previous day. As a direct course to El Adem would have taken us over the desert, and because of the turbulence, we reasoned we would be safer following the coastline again. On this leg of the journey, the visibility was once again poor and the scenery did not offer up any pleasant surprises. George did, however, make a perfect landing at El Adem, despite the turbulence and updraught from the runway. This turned out to be most fortuitous, as we discovered later that as we touched down, through no fault of ours, a Royal Air Force (RAF) jet was forced to overshoot the runway.

From the moment we arrived at the El Adem RAF base, we were treated with the utmost civility, respect and a good measure of curiosity. By this time, Charlie Golf was badly in need of an engine oil change. It was made very clear to us that we were not permitted to carry out any maintenance work on Charlie Golf while we were on the base. However, the aircraft engineers were only too pleased to oblige.

While processing the paperwork on arrival, the El Adem authorities had also stamped Charlie Golf's log book for departure and, as such, we were not permitted to leave the confines of the base.

Fortunately, we were offered accommodation within the base, which we were more than happy to accept. Only then were we informed that as there were no married quarters on the base, we would be escorted from the officers' mess to our respective singles' quarters.

We quickly freshened up, then met up again in the officers' mess for afternoon tea and toast. George took advantage of the duty-free store to replenish his king size cigarettes and bottles of Vat 69 whisky. We then returned to the bar for a drink before dining at 7.00pm. The air force officers, in fact it seemed everyone we came in contact with, were most interested and somewhat curious in both Charlie Golf and our adventures. The RAF personnel were extremely hospitable and friendly and we enjoyed one of the best meals we'd had since we left Scotland. Roast chicken, potatoes and vegetables with lashings of gravy. Having eaten our fill, it was back to the bar for more drinks and companionship. Despite being billeted separately, we sneaked my gear over to George's room and stayed the night together, there being two single beds in his billet. We didn't think anyone would have minded.

Chapter 7

Egypt

Harrowing experiences, problems and solutions

Wednesday 3 July 1968
El Adem — Alexandria, Egypt
Time of departure: 07.27 GMT Flying time: 4hrs.23mins
Flying conditions: Extremely hot with good visibility. Wind direction and velocity: 180°/05knots and 320°/15knots.

Feeling very much revived and ready to continue our travels, we rose early and breakfasted in the mess on typical English cuisine before being escorted across the base to Charlie Golf. We asked the RAF desert survival officers if we could have a decent size plastic bottle to carry drinking water on the aircraft. Much to our surprise and appreciation we were not only given the plastic bottle of water as requested, but also two fully equipped Mae West life vests (minus the homing device) and desert survival equipment, including a plastic sheet and container to make a water still from our own urine (heaven forbid) should the need arise. These items were all free of charge. The RAF base at El Adem just could not do enough for us and George and I will be forever grateful for their hospitality, consideration and companionship.

I recall one incident that really made us smile when I related it to George later.

The lecture we were given on desert safety and survival strategies, should we happen to ditch into the sea, was delivered in a classroom environment. We sat around the room on chairs with several other officers. However, one young, blond officer sat on top of a desk facing me with his knees bent and his feet on the chair in front of him. Like all other male personnel in the room, he was wearing a button-through shirt and Baden Powell shorts with wide legs. I was acutely aware that he seemed to be looking pointedly at me most of the time. Then, as soon as we made eye contact, he spread his knees and, much to my embarrassment, all his private parts were on show. Clearly, he was not wearing any underwear and I couldn't avoid getting an eyeful as he was sitting immediately in front of me and at my eye level. I quickly looked away and I don't think I was able to concentrate on the safety lecture after that. I still believe his actions were intentional and not accidental.

Once in the air flying out of El Adem, George and I had a real good laugh about it.

We found ourselves relaxed and in good humour as we followed the coastline to Alexandria. However, our comfort did not last long.

Firstly, it took us twenty minutes to locate Alexandria airport. Then, as George radioed in downwind and turned onto finals for the runway, it became apparent that air traffic control was bringing us in on a runway that had a direct cross-wind of over fifteen knots. Using all his skills, George struggled to keep Charlie Golf on the straight and level as he tried for a touchdown. Unable to keep Charlie Golf straight, he aborted the landing, opened the throttle and took off again. Fortunately, he did not overshoot the runway, but by this time we were both quite shaken. We radioed the control tower that we would be coming round for a second attempt. At the second attempt,

George nearly had Charlie Golf's wheels on the runway and then at the last second it was obvious our high-wing aircraft would not cope with the crosswind. George yanked on the throttle again and Charlie Golf left the runway sideways about two feet above the ground. I really did not think we were going to make it. The stall warning pierced the air for what seemed like an eternity before George eventually got Charlie Golf to a reasonably safe altitude again. I was absolutely terrified. I recall that at the height of the drama I heard myself yelling, 'Oh God. No!' several times.

Once back safely in the air, George, through gritted teeth, requested air traffic control for a more favourable alternative runway, preferably one that would enable us to land Charlie Golf into the wind.

To add to our distress, the only available runway was disused, covered in grass and dotted with deep potholes, but at least it had a more favourable wind direction.

Although badly shaken, and with hearts still in our mouths, I am proud to say George brought Charlie Golf down with the most perfect landing. I had tears in my eyes with relief. That had to be the scariest and most harrowing moment of our trip so far.

We will never know if it was the normal greeting given at Alexandria, but after we taxied to our parking bay on the apron, several workers came over, shook George by the hand and clapped him on the back. We like to think it was George's skilled piloting that impressed them.

Unlike Europe, a light aircraft flown by young people was a rare entity and we were beginning to attract more and more interest and curiosity the further we got into our travels. Some of the interest was genuine and positive, but, unfortunately, sometimes it was not. There was also a perception that we must be very rich to have such an aircraft and to be travelling to Australia.

The official paperwork required to be completed before we could leave the airport was no different to that required by other countries we had come through. As we filled out the necessary forms, we were bemused to notice that a very scruffy looking guard, with what looked like a rifle, had been posted beside Charlie Golf. When George returned to the aircraft to collect our personal baggage, cigarettes and alcohol, the guard, who had already been given a twenty-pack of cigarettes, grabbed for another two packets. Only when George yelled out to him did he drop them.

Feeling somewhat uneasy, we hired a taxi and asked to be taken to a cheap hotel in the city. The taxi driver's idea of a cheap hotel turned out to be a magnificent building surrounded with luscious gardens and located on the sea front. With plush red carpets and Arab clientele wearing flowing, pure white robes with blue or gold trimmings, it was obviously not going to be a cheap night. To make matters worse, the taxi driver tried to cheat us out of quite a lot of money and it took a heated argument and a great deal of gesticulating before George finally got it back.

Our room for the night was extremely luxurious with double balcony, air-conditioning and en-suite shower, bath and toilet, and, oh yes, two single beds again. The view over the blue green waters of the Mediterranean was quite magnificent and after a day of hot, dusty travelling, all I wanted to do was to go for a cool swim. With this in mind, I left George at the hotel bar and made my way to the nearest swimming spot.

It never occurred to me that I would be asked to pay and, as I had no Egyptian currency with me, I had to return to the hotel bitterly disappointed. In a bad frame of mind, I decided to get on with the day's chores instead.

At around 8.00pm, George and I stepped out from the hotel for a leisurely walk to take in the sights, sounds and smells of Alexandria and to add some more photos and movies to our collection. Because it was so hot, I wore the short-sleeved, cotton dress. Once out on the street, it became blatantly obvious that my casual and comfortable attire was definitely not appropriate in this part of the world. We had only gone a few hundred yards from the hotel entrance when we became aware that we were being hassled and followed too closely for our comfort by a group of young males. One started to touch and paw my shoulder-length, blond hair, while another ducked down to look up my skirt. By this time, I was beginning to feel vulnerable and quite anxious. George began mouthing off and yelling at them in anger. Before the melee got any worse, I grabbed George's arm and turned back for the hotel. Once there, I changed into my daggy jeans and shapeless shirt that I wore when we were flying. I also tightly tied my hair up into a ponytail and caught it into the nape of my neck.

We cautiously ventured onto the streets again and even though we were still a curiosity, we did not attract the same amount of attention as before. After that experience, every time we ventured out in Egypt, I always tried to look my daggiest and least feminine. After a cautious short walk that night, we ate a four course meal at the hotel before retiring.

—

Thursday 4 July
Alexandria — Cairo, Egypt

Time of departure: 06.37 GMT   Flying time: 1hr 45mins
Flying conditions: Clear skies, poor visibility due to haze.
Wind direction and velocity: 340°/10knots.

That morning the diary indicated that we rose at 7.00am.

Despite a good night's sleep, I was still very tired and, probably because of our experiences the previous day, I was not looking forward to climbing into Charlie Golf for another day's flying. Surprisingly enough, we cleared the officialdom at Alexandria quite quickly and made an incident free take off to Cairo.

I was quite excited about visiting Cairo. As a child I was fascinated with pictures of the pyramids, the sphinx, camels and palm trees along the Nile. At one point in my schooling, I even considered archaeology as a career.

Despite the low level mist, we were relaxed but alert with our flying regime and able to enjoy the contrast in scenery between the lush green vegetation along the river and the orange sand of the desert on the horizon.

As we picked up the radio frequency on our approach to Cairo, it became blatantly obvious that this was the busiest international airport which we had to land at so far on our travels. The traffic was extreme and we sighted at least six passenger jets as we approached at the designated altitude of 3,000ft. Regardless, all went well and George brought us in through the traffic to a perfect landing. Once on the tarmac, it took us about twenty minutes to taxi to our allotted parking bay. As we were refuelling Charlie Golf, George discovered a small tear in the seam next to the fuel tank on the right wing. The tear would have to be repaired before we could fly again.

After reporting to flight control, we were once again shuffled back and forth from one official to the other until we were absolutely sick and tired of the whole procedure. We were repeatedly called on to explain who we were, why we were in their country, what we intended to do in their country, why we wanted to fly to our next destination, and why we were not travelling by conventional passenger jet. And so it went on ...

This time heated discussions took place regarding regulations that required us to seal or make secure Charlie Golf, as the doors to the cockpit had no locks, the windows were Perspex and the wings were canvas. It was just simply impossible to seal the aircraft. Eventually, after sorting out that problem to our mutual satisfaction, we were told to report to the Transit Director.

The Transit Director duly informed us that it was not possible to proceed to Amman by our intended route via Hurghad and Aqaba. Because of the Israeli-Egyptian conflict it meant we would be flying over extremely sensitive military operations and would be in danger of being shot down. We were absolutely gutted. This could mean our trip to Australia would come to an abrupt end right here in Cairo. Trying to contain our anger and disappointment— we'd come too far and experienced too much to give up now—we discussed the options. We were also warned that on no account must we land in Israel. To do so would mean that no other Arab state would allow us into or through their country regardless of the circumstances. It soon became apparent the only alternative route would be to fly direct from Cairo to Beirut, fly over the mountains into Damascus and Amman, then re-join our original planned route along the oil pipe line through Saudi Arabia.

The difficulty with this was that we were unable to check the viability of following such a route as we did not possess topographical maps of the region and therefore had no way of calculating exact distances.

By this time we were hot, tired, frustrated, angry, and in very bad humour. It felt like the odds and the world were constantly stacking up against us. I was getting truly fed up with having to fight the system every step of the way and it was beginning to show.

When we realised there was nothing more we could do,

we decided to mull over our options when we were in a better frame of mind and able to think more clearly. So we took a taxi into Cairo and for once were relieved to discover the taxi driver knew the meaning of a "reasonably cheap" hotel. He took us to the Capsis Palace Hotel. It wasn't flash, but it was comfortable and met our immediate needs.

After a wash, followed by a few drinks, we came to the conclusion that our first step was to try and get some maps that covered the region between Cairo, Beirut and Amman. That decision made, and feeling like we had a regained some control over our destiny, we ventured out onto the streets of Cairo to do some shopping and sightseeing. The hubbub of the Cairo metropolis was all very new and somewhat overwhelming for us. For a start, the intricacy of arguing and haggling over prices was totally foreign to our British culture and we were really uncomfortable with it. We always had the sense that we were being cheated and, until we got used to the concept, it raised feelings of anger. The public transport system was another eye-opener. Every bus and tram was packed with people hanging out of the windows and clinging to the roof, sides, front and the back of every dirty, dilapidated vehicle. There did not appear to be any road rules, with cars, motor bikes, cycles and other modes of transport juggling for space on the crowded roads. The sound of beeping horns and ringing bicycle bells was continuous. To add to this, we were amazed at the number of soldiers on the streets. They were everywhere. It seemed the pavements were lined with men in uniform trying to cadge a lift from the passing vehicles. Similarly, we found it difficult to come to terms with the way adolescent boys and grown men held hands or linked arms when they walked with each other. This was really alien to Scottish culture. We also had to get used to being followed and being the butt of people's curiosity.

We eventually found a restaurant we felt met our hygiene standards and ordered lamb kebabs roasted over charcoal and served with sweet-tasting rice. Being 1968, this was not the type of food we were used to and George had real difficulty coping with it. On the other hand, I thoroughly enjoyed the new taste.

We walked back to our modest hotel somewhat drunk and very tired.

—

Friday 5 July
Cairo, Egypt

I didn't sleep very well at all that night due to the continual noise coming up from the streets and the heat. Oh, God! We'd never experienced such heat before. We didn't get out of bed 'til 10.00. George disappeared down to the hotel bar and came back with iced beers and Cokes for breakfast. I then carried out the usual chores of washing, writing cards, etcetera, while George sun-baked on the balcony and drank beer. Chores done, we showered and went to the Hilton Hotel to cash some traveller's cheques.

We had decided earlier that our best strategy at this point in time was to seek the assistance of the British Embassy staff and ask if they were able to provide us with the appropriate topographical maps that would enable us to continue on the next leg of our journey.

The taxi driver got us to the embassy without any incidents. Once there, we were told that the British Air Attaché was on leave, but, fortunately, Colonel De Butt, the Military Attaché was sympathetic to our plight and took us under his wing. He was able to provide us with several maps that adequately suited our purpose.

In addition to providing us with maps, Colonel De Butt

offered us the services of his driver to take us to the bazaars the following morning to try and locate the dope George needed to repair the tear in Charlie Golf's wing. For the record, 'dope' is not the drug that is commonly smoked today, but lacquer that, when painted over the canvas, had the effect of shrinking the canvas taut to form a smooth, tight skin, allowing air to flow over the wing.

Feeling like we were once more in control of our destiny, we lunched on sandwiches and afterwards took a siesta in our hotel room for a couple of hours. In the early evening we again went for a walk onto the busy Cairo streets. The performance of the previous evening was repeated. We were followed by groups of men, sneered at, and, although we could not understand the language, were left in no doubt that the loud comments made as we passed by were not complimentary. We started to tire of the attention, and so after taking a few more photos and movie film of the Nile and its surrounds, we called it quits and headed back to the hotel for an evening meal.

As we entered the foyer, a group of young men standing close by made comments and one young man attempted to touch my hair. That was the last straw for George and he let fly at them with a mouthful of verbal abuse as only a Scotsman can when riled.

We were five minutes into our dinner when another young man from the same group came over to George and apologised on behalf of the others. He then invited us to join them for a drink after we had finished our meal. We had just put our knives down when the youth returned to our table and suggested we go upstairs with him to join his friends. I did not like this idea at all and George was none too keen either. As we were dithering over how to politely refuse, the hotel restaurant manager resolved the matter for us. In an extremely quiet, but very persuasive manner, he gently told the group of young men to leave the hotel. He then warned George and me not to speak to, or give anything over to these types of youths who congregate in gangs. We appreciated the manager's intervention and advice. By this time we were on edge and had had enough for the day, so we returned to our sixth floor room where I wrote a long letter home before retiring to bed.

—

Saturday 6 July
Cairo, Egypt

On waking that morning, I was depressed to realise we were still in Cairo and going nowhere. As previously arranged, we returned to the British Embassy at 9.00am to meet the Colonel's driver. Before we left in the Colonel's car, he very kindly invited us to have lunch with him and his wife after we returned from our shopping expedition. We gladly accepted. The embassy driver understood exactly what George was looking for to enable him to successfully carry out the repair work. At the second paint shop, George purchased dope-type lacquer, not exactly what was wanted but an excellent substitute. We parted company with the driver at the British Embassy and George and I walked back to our hotel. On the way, we were appalled and nauseated to see an adult male squat in the gutter and defecate. Others in the close vicinity took absolutely no notice, so we assumed it was not an uncommon occurrence. All of this against the backdrop of magnificent white buildings with lush gardens. I must say we found the contradiction between wealth and opulence and filth and squalor quite overwhelming and extremely difficult to comprehend.

I also recall the street urchins running beside us with their grubby hands held out, begging for money. They always seemed to be smiling. I was also amazed at how the women could tolerate the heat with such heavy fabric draped on their bodies and see where they were walking with the webbed material covering their faces. Although in our mid-twenties, this was the first time we had encountered the *burqa* worn by some women of the Muslim faith.

We freshened up in the hotel and then at 1.00pm returned to the British Embassy to meet Colonel De Butt as arranged. The driver transported the three of us to the Colonel's flat located close to the Embassy. On arrival, his wife gave us the warmest of welcomes and we immediately felt very much at ease.

We spent about half an hour partaking of pre-dinner drinks and talking with the Colonel and his wife. A dark-skinned, Egyptian servant then ushered us into the luxurious dining room where we were served a delicious mid-day meal of roast beef and roast potatoes with all the trimmings. Feeling quite full, we retired to yet another room where we continued to converse over coffee. The De Butts were fascinated by, and showed a great interest in, our travel experiences. In turn, George and I were given an insight into the diplomatic world of politics and intrigue of the Middle East as related by the Colonel. Colonel De Butt very kindly provided us with a written reference to introduce us to his friend and colleague in Sharjah when we eventually got there.

It was late afternoon by the time the Embassy driver returned us to the Capsis Palace Hotel.

Despite the hour, George decided to go out to the airport to check on Charlie Golf, repair the split in the wing and to work out a flight plan for our onward journey. I stayed behind and caught up with the chores. He returned to the hotel at around 8.00pm having carried out a successful repair to the canvas of Charlie Golf's right wing. On speaking with the aviation authorities, he learned that the flying distance from Cairo to Beirut was 350nautical miles. A distance well and truly beyond Charlie Golf's fuel range.

George always managed to come up with the most ingenious and inventive ideas when his back was against the wall. This time was no different. He would not accept that we were beaten. Instead, he worked out that the extra fuel needed to cover the distance would be about a large container full. Thinking laterally, he reasoned that if we could somehow refuel the belly tank while using the fuel in the wing tanks we could conceivably get to Beirut. His solution was to purchase a flexible hose, a funnel and a large plastic container, fill the container with avgas and fuel Charlie Golf mid-flight.

I was dumbfounded.

Charlie Golf has one belly tank slung under the body of the aircraft and a fuel tank on each wing. George's reasoning was simple. He would remove the joystick from my side of the controls to enable me to sit with a container full of avgas on my knee. We would fly the first section of the trip using the fuel in the belly tank until it was almost empty then switch over to the fuel in the wing tanks. George would insert the hose into the belly tank and while holding it steady, I would put the funnel in the exposed end of the hose and tip the fuel from the container into the funnel, down the hose and into the belly tank. Once all the fuel was transferred from the container to the tank, he would then switch back to using the fuel in the belly tank, thus preserve the remaining fuel in the wing tanks. The cap replaced on the tank, we would then resume normal flying. By George's calculations, this simple, but extremely dangerous, manoeuvre would give us precious additional flying time and should get us to Beirut.

I was far from happy about this procedure, but could see

the possibilities. Anyway, it was either that or give up and go back to Scotland.

The next day being Sunday, and with all the shops closed, we realised that we could not hunt for the gear we needed until Monday. This meant we would have to sit tight in Cairo for at least another two days.

As if matters couldn't be worse, both George and I had contracted a good dose of diarrhoea.

—

Sunday 7 July
Cairo, Egypt

Despite the stomach ailment, George rose early and returned to the airport to cancel the flying arrangements he had made the previous day. I, however, stayed in bed 'til late morning. When George got back to the hotel, I knew he had had a few drinks and I just collapsed into a blubbering heap. By this time I was sick of the never-ending problems and extremely homesick and fearful of the future. I also couldn't understand why my husband needed to drink alcohol in the middle of the day. However, like him, I have a stubborn streak and the thought of returning to Scotland as a failure was worse than the prospect of continuing the journey, albeit with the inherent dangers.

Thus, we decided it was time to make the most of our situation and get out and about to see the wonders that ancient Egypt had to offer.

After getting the necessary information from the hotel reception desk and once more attired in our daggiest garb, we made our way to the bus station and climbed aboard a number 119 bus to take us to the pyramids and the sphinx. As was the norm in Cairo, the bus was absolutely packed with passengers. As we got underway, I began to feel quite ill with the heat, the diesel fumes and the claustrophobic conditions on the bus, so much so that I felt myself passing out. Fortunately, George managed to catch me. Another passenger, realising the situation, quickly got me to a seat with an open window. Although still uncomfortable, I was able to cope after that.

When we alighted the bus at Giza, we were quickly joined by a very well dressed English speaking Arab gentleman with a walking stick. He offered to be our guide. George and I did not have money to spend on the official tours, so we decided to take the risk and go with him. He led us down the somewhat dirty and smelly back streets of the village of Giza and up a short incline. This took us to the tombs of the priests and servants of the kings who were buried in the pyramids. He was extremely knowledgeable and fascinating to listen to. We found ourselves trusting and warming to the old man. Feeling thirsty, the three of us returned to the village and sat on the roadside to freshen up with cold beers. He told us that at 8.00pm there would be a spectacular display whereby the sphinx would be lit with spotlights and the story of Egypt related to the audience over a loudspeaker. The cost of entry was £2 each. George and I couldn't afford that sort of money so our companion told us to meet him at 8.00pm at a mutually agreed place and he would take us to a spot where we would be able to see and hear the spectacle at no cost.

Once again on our own, George and I headed off to explore the pyramids. Seeing that we were unaccompanied, two much less respectable and trustworthy looking Arabs, one with a horse, the other with a camel, immediately pounced on us and offered to show us the sights. After much haggling over the price, George climbed up on the camel and I mounted the horse. We spent about an hour taking in the wonders of the pyramids and surrounds. On the way back, we swapped over and I rode the camel and George the horse. We laughed at how ridiculous we must have looked. It was good to have fun after the stress of recent days.

As always, we had a dispute with our tour guides. This time it was about the amount of change George had due to him. We eventually resolved the matter before entering the restaurant for much needed refreshments. We finished eating and as we made our way to meet the Arab gentleman, we took the opportunity to take numerous photographs and movie film. Meeting up once again, we skulled another beer before retracing our steps through the village back-streets to the base of a sandy hill that overlooked the sphinx and the pyramids. Another elderly man offered to take me to the top on his donkey for about five piastres. Why not? It added to the fun and the atmosphere. We did get to the top, but at the halfway mark the donkey decided to get difficult and refused to go any further. We had locals pushing, the Arab gentleman pulling, and the old donkey owner beating the beast, before it would continue the climb. I felt sorry for the animal and wanted to get off and walk, but the locals wouldn't have any of it and I had to stay on.

It was all worthwhile. We reached the top as the late afternoon turned to dusk. Spread out before us was the most splendid spectacle we had yet seen. The magnificent, huge, brilliant red sun was slowly setting behind the pyramids. It was breathtaking and we eagerly used up lots of film. As night fell and the dark set in, the whole place lit up with different coloured spotlights. Male and female voices gave a running commentary on the history of the pyramids and the sphinx in sync with beautiful music and the changing lights. The entire experience was quite spectacular and quite romantic.

By the time the show ended we were both emotionally revived but very tired. As we boarded the bus back to Cairo,

George gave our self-appointed guide ten shillings to show our respect and appreciation for taking us under his wing and giving us such a wonderful experience.

Both of us still felt a little squeamish when we got back to the hotel, but we ate a bowl of hot soup thinking it would help, but it didn't. We went to bed feeling quite unwell.

—

Monday 8 July
Cairo, Egypt

Monday morning we were still in Cairo and George was still feeling decidedly unwell, whereas I felt much better. While I washed out some clothes in the en suite sink, George took off for the bazaar to locate a hose, funnel and plastic container we would need for our mid-air fuelling stunt. He was gone for ages and as I was growing concerned. I sat in the hotel foyer awaiting his return. When he finally got back, he was exhausted. Apparently, he had located a plastic container, but at the same time he had attracted the unsolicited attention of a seedy looking Arab. In a bid to shake off the unwanted follower, apparently George ducked down a couple of alleyways and made his way back to the hotel without having purchased the container. After a drink to refresh and revive him, the two of us ventured back to the stall in the bazaar. Firstly we needed to change a traveller's cheque for some ready cash. This was always easier said than done. Being more street-wise, we eventually located a street stall owner who cashed the cheque for a better value than that given by the banks. What were we becoming? Now we were dabbling in the "black market". George found the stall that sold the plastic container and, after much haggling, bought it at what seemed a reasonable price.

At another stall we bought two drinks of freshly squeezed orange juice to relieve our thirst.

I must admit there were many things I would have loved to have bought in those markets: carved figurines; beautiful colourful fabrics; intricately patterned silk rugs; small tables carved from rich, dark wood; beaded bags and shoes; and aromatic soaps and perfumes. Unfortunately, we could not afford to buy knick-knacks and, anyway, we had no space in Charlie Golf to carry them.

It took us four hours of searching before we eventually tracked down a piece of hose and a suitably sized funnel. By this time we were absolutely exhausted.

During our wanderings, we somehow came across a small café-type restaurant down a side alley where we were delighted to dine on large helpings of pasta and pizza pies.

As we dined, we discussed our options, deciding it would be best if we got a good night's sleep, take it easy the following day, then leave Cairo at first light on Wednesday morning. Later, while sitting at the bar in the hotel, we befriended Hugh Jacobs, a Canadian guy who happened to be touring the Middle East in a small Citroen. Hugh, himself a holder of a private pilot's licence, very kindly offered to drive us out to the airport the following day. George and I hit the sack at about 11.00, but, despite our best intentions, neither of us slept well. I believe it was due to a combination of the overwhelming anxiety and the intense heat and humidity.

—

Tuesday 9 July
Cairo, Egypt

Considering what we had to look forward to over the next couple of days, it was not surprising that George and I both failed to get the night's rest we had hoped for. By mid-day, we had completed our chores, showered and packed all the gear.

We vacated the room and paid the hotel bill before meeting up with Hugh in the bar at the pre-arranged time. Having nothing else to do to occupy ourselves, we sat drinking with Hugh for a couple of hours and passed the time exchanging flying experiences.

After obtaining the relevant information on the weather and radio frequencies, we filed our flight plan for dawn the following morning. That night we planned to sleep rough in the airport in order to get the earliest start possible. Some of our free time was spent showing Hugh the workings of Charlie Golf.

At 7.00pm, the three of us headed back into Cairo for a meal at the same side street restaurant and cafe in which we had previously eaten. We really enjoyed our meal and it seemed there was no subject that we could not mull over with Hugh. Later that evening he drove us back to Cairo International Airport and we said our farewells. George did some final checks on Charlie Golf and then we settled down in the airport lounge and read as many English language newspapers as we could find.

The airport lounges had emptied of regular travellers by the early hours of the morning, so George and I were left to join the many Egyptian airport staff sleeping in bedrolls on chairs, benches, ledges and on the floor. Dossing in Cairo International Airport was obviously a very normal way to spend the night. The diary indicates that perhaps George and I managed to get about one hour's sleep.

Chapter 8

Beirut

Mid-flight fuel top up and a sick pilot

Wednesday 10 July 1968
Cairo — Beirut, Lebanon
Time of departure: 03.10 GMT Flying time: 5hrs 21mins
Flying conditions: Low cloud near coast, poor visibility.
Wind direction and velocity: 300°/20knots.

That day's flight was to be one of the worst we would experience.

Before the dawn take-off, George made sure we had packed all the necessary gear that would enable us to add fuel to the belly tank in mid-flight. I sat in my seat with the large plastic container containing approximately five gallons (twenty-two litres) of avgas on my knee. The joystick from the controls on my side of the aircraft had been detached and was on top of the luggage in the rear seat. This was how we took off for Beirut and not one of the airport staff questioned the safety aspects of this set-up.

We left Cairo International Airport without incident. Flight regulations required us to follow a route that took us north to the Mediterranean coast, report our position over Baltim on the coast, then set a heading direct for Lebanon.

The flight to Baltim was slow and took longer than expected. It was on this section of the trip that George started to feel ill.

We reported over Baltim as required and altered our heading for the trip to Beirut.

Because of the dense sea mist, we had no clearly defined horizon and so flying conditions out over the sea were extremely poor.

As Charlie Golf was not equipped with a fuel gauge that gave a reading for the belly tank, we had to make our own calculations to determine when it was nearing empty. When we believed we had used up as much of the fuel as was safely possible, George switched over to the wing tanks and we proceeded to carry out the strategic process of in-flight refuelling. George opened the door on his side of the aircraft and with his shoulder held it ajar against the slipstream. He then reached down and unscrewed the cap off the fuel tank and brought it inside. I passed him the hose pipe and held one end while he fed the other end down into the belly tank. The external wind pressure on the door held the hose securely in place. I then handed him the other end of the hose pipe with the funnel firmly jammed in the top. As he held the hose steady I precariously tipped the avgas into the funnel and down into the tank. At first some fuel spilled over us. However, I soon got the pour under control and we managed to successfully transfer the five gallons of avgas into the belly tank. Once the container was empty, George removed the hose from the belly tank and replaced the cap. He then switched from using the fuel in the wing tanks, back to the fuel in the belly tank. I tossed the hose, funnel and container onto the back seat. This whole manoeuvre was done with George gripping the joystick on his side of the aircraft between his knees to keep Charlie Golf on course and flying straight and level. Finally, I opened all the air vents to get rid of the overpowering avgas fumes.

Although the refuelling was successful, our troubles continued.

Given the flying conditions and lack of obvious horizon, George was finding it harder and harder to focus. Keeping Charlie Golf on straight and level and on the correct compass heading was becoming progressively difficult as his nausea and dizziness worsened. He was obviously very ill, but, fortunately, I was able to take control of Charlie Golf when the circumstances required. He later admitted to hallucinating and seeing false horizons.

To add yet another dimension to these dramas, the Beagle Terrier single-engine aircraft is more or less the sister-craft to the Auster. Aircraft enthusiasts would know that the Auster is regularly used by military and air defence as a spotter plane, or spy aircraft. As Egypt and Israel were at war, for us to fly such an aircraft from Egypt, heading towards Lebanon along the Israeli coastline was asking to be intercepted or shot down by Israeli forces. Thus we stayed out over the sea as far away from the coast for as long as was practical. However, because of the state George was in and the unwavering sea mist, we decided that to alter course, find and follow the coastline, was the lesser of the two evils. At this point in the journey we reckoned we were approximately two hours from our estimated time of arrival into Beirut.

By this time we were both in a state of panic. The coastline seemed to elude us, although we were absolutely certain we were on the correct course. We were well and truly eating up the fuel in the wing tanks when we noticed a slight shift in the weather conditions. White, fluffy clouds were forming at about two thousand feet. I felt sure this had to be a sign of land close by. Lo and behold, the coast appeared on our starboard side. Relief was welcome but short-lived. I now had to plot our exact position. Oh, God! Could it get any worse? We were flying up the Israeli coast approximately two or three miles south of Haifa.

The likelihood of being shot at had increased tenfold. This did not improve our morale one bit.

Not to be daunted, we trekked up the coast listening intently to every beat of Charlie Golf's Gypsy Major Ten engine and just waiting for that first splutter that would indicate an empty fuel tank. At the same time, we were watching the landscape intently for an alternative airfield. We reasoned that there may be one on the Lebanese side of the border where the oil pipeline met the coast. No such luck.

By this time, our starboard wing tank indicated we had one gallon remaining and the port wing tank indicated three gallons. Now we really were panicking and praying for nothing less than a miracle. Even George, who normally thrived on these challenges, was showing the stress and strain.

At last some relief. We had radio contact with Beirut, so we requested, or perhaps begged, for a straight-in approach due to lack of fuel. Recognising the gravity of our situation, the air traffic controller on duty immediately cleared the runways of all other traffic and granted a straight-in approach for Charlie Golf. Just to see the airfield brought absolute overwhelming feelings of relief. Despite this, my mind was racing. I was going over and over in my head the procedures for landing Charlie Golf, should George pass out and I was forced to bring the aircraft down solo.

By this time we had stopped looking at the fuel tank gauges as they all indicated just about empty. We were now listening to every beat of that engine up front.

The final approach to the runway of Beirut Airport took us directly over the sky scrapers and high-rise buildings of the city. If Charlie Golf's engine had conked out at that point, it would have been an unmitigated disaster and our days would have been over. Once at the airport perimeter, it was an immediate descent onto the runway.

Amazingly, George, as sick and disorientated as he was, executed a perfect landing. The feeling of elation and relief was unimaginable. We had just completed a total flying time of five hours and twenty-one minutes and, with the starboard fuel gauge reading empty and the port fuel gauge reading one-and-a-half gallons, we had just enough left to enable us to taxi to the nearest apron.

By this time, George was in a real bad state. He could hardly stand and he looked like death. Fortunately, the airport officials, recognising our plight, hastily and efficiently managed our airport clearance. As soon as we could, we collapsed into a taxi and booked ourselves into a hotel in the city of Beirut.

The hotel was clean, bright, light and comfortable with a very efficient air conditioner. Heaven! Now that I had the luxury to assess George's condition, it was blatantly obvious he was running a dangerously high temperature. I reasoned that he needed plenty to drink and a good, well-earned sleep, so I bundled him into bed between crisp, white, cotton sheets. Given it was still only mid-morning — our arrival time in Beirut was approximately 08.45 — I decided to do some washing while George slept. The hotel housekeeper was most kind and offered to hang the washing out to dry on the terracing. I then also collapsed into bed for a much needed sleep.

That sleep was the best I'd had for the past six or seven nights. I woke at 5.00pm to the distressing noise of George throwing up again in the bathroom. His temperature was still up and he was now quite delirious. I encouraged him to drink more water and return to bed.

As I was now wide awake, I completed some of our other chores, showered and dressed. I didn't want to leave George alone for too long, so I went out for a short walk and did some window shopping. The shops were a very pleasant surprise after our experiences of the past week and I was able to buy a British magazine as well as the usual postcards to send home. I made my way back to the hotel with my treasures, ate a simple meal in a nearby restaurant, then returned to our room. George was still running a temperature, but his condition seemed stable, so I decided that bed was the best place for me too.

I fell asleep thinking about how friendly and helpful the Lebanese people had been and how clean and picturesque the city of Beirut was. I loved the way the high-rise buildings stood out against the backdrop of beautiful, lush green and snow-capped mountains. A stark contrast to the Cairo we had just left.

—

Thursday 11 July
Beirut, Lebanon

At around 6.00am, George's ablutions woke me from a very deep and restful sleep. However, I was able to fall back to sleep and didn't wake again til 9.00am. My first task was to start planning our next leg of the journey and to set the wheels in motion for obtaining authorisation to enter Syria, Jordan and Saudi Arabia so that we could follow the oil pipe line across the desert.

George was feeling a little better by this time, but still had severe stomach cramps. I reasoned that he had contracted a hefty dose of food poisoning while in Cairo. After he freshened up and was comfortably back in bed, I left him on his own to recuperate.

My first stop was the Mobil Oil offices of Beirut to seek permission to fly along the Trans Arabian Oil pipeline and to use the airfields on the way. I learned that Mobil did not operate the pipeline. I was advised I would need to speak to the public relations officer of Trans Arabian Tapline.

This officer more or less laughed in my face. Apparently, permission to fly along the pipeline had to be obtained from the Governments through which the pipeline runs. Further, as the Trans Arabian Tapline company's own aircraft were not permitted to fly over Syria, he could not envisage us, as British citizens, being given authorisation. I think this gentleman's smirking negative attitude must have got me riled as the diary notes indicate, *I told him in no uncertain terms that we would not be put off that easily. We then parted company.*

My next stop was to talk our problem over with the air traffic controllers at Beirut Airport. The controller I spoke to was extremely helpful and suggested we send a wire to the aviation authorities of Syria, Jordan and Saudi Arabia seeking permission to fly Charlie Golf down the pipeline. He believed we would not be refused. However, he warned me that we may have to fly to Damascus and Amman before joining the pipeline over Turayf. The wire sent and paid for, I jumped into a taxi and returned to the hotel. The air traffic controller promised to telephone me at the hotel as soon as he received a response to the wire.

Back in our room, George's condition was slowly improving, but he was still far from well. Despite this, he managed to keep down a beef sandwich and Coke, his first food in two days.

With the pressure and stress now easing, and being a sucker for the sun and sea, I left George to rest some more and went down to the local beach. There I allowed myself the luxury of relaxing in the sun on a deck chair and swimming in the beautiful lukewarm green-blue waters of the Mediterranean. After two hours, I returned to our room to find George much more improved. As I was having a shower, the air traffic controller rang requesting our intended departure date from Beirut. George told him we expected to leave on 13 July, weather and flying conditions permitting.

With George still feeling rather squeamish, at about 8.30pm I went back out on my own to eat. This time I went into a small café-type restaurant next door to the hotel. Finding a corner table, I ordered a Steak Dianne and a Coca Cola to drink. While I was enjoying my meal the owner of the cafe, a tall, dark, handsome and very charming man of about thirty years of age came over to me and apologised for passing remarks to me when I walked by his establishment earlier in the afternoon. This incident is not noted in the diary and so I am unable to make comment on both his supposed remarks or my reaction to them. However, I did accept his apology. He then asked me to lunch with him the following day. I respectfully declined explaining that I was married and that my husband was in the hotel recuperating from a bout of food poisoning. He said he wanted to buy me a salad to accompany my steak. I once more refused, but thanked him. Five minutes later a salad was placed on my table. As I finished my meal, he returned to the table and introduced himself as Erika and asked me if he could buy me a drink. This time I accepted, and he sat at the table while we both enjoyed an orange liqueur. We spent the next hour or so discussing the war, Lebanese and British culture, and the beauty of Beirut. When I rose to leave, he would not allow me to pay for my meal. To my surprise, he also suggested I ask George's permission to accompany him to a Lebanese nightclub. I flatly refused, telling him it was absolutely out of the question. By this time George, feeling much better, was growing concerned at my absence. However, when I told him I had scored a free feed, he was quite pleased and didn't seem to mind that I had been propositioned. I'd had a real busy and interesting day so I was very pleased to retire for the night.

—

Friday 12 July
Beirut, Lebanon

This morning George was feeling a great deal better, so we splashed out and ordered room service continental breakfast, which we both thoroughly enjoyed. After we freshened up, the two of us took a leisurely stroll along the beach, but George quickly tired with the effort. Obviously he hadn't regained his lost energy. While we were walking, we happened to meet one of the airport officials who had supported us when we first landed in Beirut. He asked after George's welfare and, after chatting for a few minutes, he and his friend offered to pick us up at the hotel at 2.00pm to take us up the mountains on a sightseeing tour. We gladly accepted.

Our new acquaintances — the diary identifies the driver as Ameen — arrived at the hotel at the appointed time and we headed up a very windy road to a restaurant through the most magnificent scenery. The lush, panoramic views reminded George and I of the time we spent in Switzerland a few years earlier. Looking down the mountainside from our table in the restaurant, we could just see the runways of Beirut airport, sometimes slightly obscured by the rising heat haze. As we sat and talked, we were treated to a sumptuous lunch of roast lamb kebabs, salads, fruit, nuts and sauerkraut.

Feeling very satisfied, relaxed and content, we were dropped back at the hotel at 4.30pm with the promise that Ameen would send a car for us the following morning at 6.30am to take us to Beirut Airport. We rested in our room, then went for a walk when darkness set in. Being unable to find an eating place that suited our purposes, we returned to Erika's cafe. I introduced George to Erika and we ordered a pasta meal. No sooner had our plates arrived, than the waiter brought a bottle of red wine to the table, compliments of the proprietor. Erika joined us at the table again, but we didn't linger for long as we still had chores and packing to complete before the next day's flight.

Chapter 9

Syria

Hair-raising take-off and desert flying

Saturday 13 July 1968
Beirut — Damascus, Syria
Time of departure: 08.57 GMT Flying time: 2hrs 01min
Flying conditions: Good visibility, poor conditions for climbing. Wind direction and velocity: 300°/10knots.

As promised, the car was waiting to take us to the airport at 6.30am. However, more problems awaited us when we got there. Why were we not surprised?

Air traffic control told us that because of the war we were not permitted to fly direct to Amman. Instead we had to fly over Damascus, then zigzag our way over the desert, reporting in over several compass points on the way. We were also told that no British or American aircraft were permitted to land in, or overfly, Syria. We were not comfortable with the new instructions as once again it was bordering on the limit of Charlie Golf's range. By the time we mulled over the problem it was 10.00am and hot. Nevertheless, we made the decision to take the risk and go. We did, however, register ourselves as Scottish Nationals on the flight plan.

To clear the mountain range surrounding Beirut, and also to comply with aviation regulations, we had to fly at an altitude of 8,000ft. George took Charlie Golf over the sea, then began a laborious upward spiral until we reached the required altitude.

Because of the heat, this manoeuvre took over forty-five minutes of our precious time and fuel. To add to our dilemma, we found ourselves in Damascus air space quite unexpectedly and much sooner than we anticipated. Because of the additional time taken to reach 8,000ft, we now found it absolutely necessary to land and refuel at Damascus.

As we approached Damascus airport, the radio controller asked us to identify ourselves. George responded with, 'This is Golf Alpha Sierra Charlie Golf en route to Amman requesting permission to refuel at Damascus.'

There was a definite pause before the controller came back with, 'Say again your call sign.' George again replied, 'This is Golf Alpha Sierra Charlie Golf en route to Amman requesting permission to refuel at Damascus.'

Another pause.

The controller then said, 'Charlie Golf, please confirm that you are an Irish registered aircraft with a Scottish pilot.'

George, realising it was time to come clean, said, 'Negative. We are British citizens and the aircraft is British registered.'

Yet another pause.

Then, 'Charlie Golf, you must not, I say again, must not, land at Damascus. You must proceed to Amman.'

George and I looked at each other with horror. He explained to the controller that we did not have enough fuel in our tanks to proceed to Amman.

The instruction was given to return to Beirut. Unbelievably, at that exact moment, Charlie Golf's generator warning light came on.

Now George was able to respond, with all honesty, that we

also had an emergency on board and as such, had no choice but to land in Damascus.

Thankfully, we were granted an emergency 'straight in' approach landing into Damascus.

We couldn't believe it! This was the first time we had experienced any mechanical problems and it occurred exactly at that moment. It was almost as if Charlie Golf was human.

After we landed, it was quite apparent that we were certainly not welcome in Syria. As we walked across the tarmac from the aircraft to the control tower, we were closely followed by two Syrian soldiers pointing their automatic weapons at our backs. We were very lucky the Syrians hadn't decided it would be easier to shoot us down.

Fortunately, George was able to fix the generator quite quickly and we were permitted to refuel. However, we were instructed to immediately leave Damascus and Syrian air space. Because of the heat, George tried to persuade the authorities to allow us to fly out later in the day, but they insisted that we leave immediately the refuelling procedure was complete.

Chapter 10

Jordan

Bounces, ground loops and heart-warming hospitality

Saturday 13 July 1968
Damascus – Amman, Jordan
Time of departure: 13.37 GMT Flying time: 2hrs 53mins
Flying conditions: Hot, turbulent, poor conditions for climbing. Wind direction and velocity: 290°/15knots.

Damascus Airport is approximately 3,000ft above mean sea level and our time of departure was 15.30, about the hottest part of the day and with no updraught rising from the runway.

Charlie Golf, with a maximum fuel load, almost refused to lift off the runway. George opened up the throttle as we rolled down the very long runway. Our trusty aircraft bounced several times then lifted a few feet off the tarmac. We skimmed across the top of the grass at the end of the runway and, with the stall warning screeching continuously, just managed to avoid a telegraph pole. George flew Charlie Golf under the power lines and over the perimeter fence, clearing it by only metres.

By this time, my nerves were absolutely shot and I had to work hard to keep my terror in check. After all, I still had to navigate across the desert.

Interestingly, as we were flying over Damascus Airport, we

couldn't help but notice the rows of wrecked military aircraft lying next to the runways and hangars. I guess this was yet another reason why we were not welcome in Syria.

We were fully aware that Damascus air traffic control had us on radar for the entire trip to Amman, but, despite our nervous anxiety, my navigation was spot-on and, as required, we radioed in over the reporting beacons on time.

To minimise the effect of the wind, we travelled across the volcanic terrain at an altitude of approximately 200ft. However, doing so had its dangers. Not far from Damascus airport, we encountered a strong updraught that took us from 200ft to 1500ft in seconds. As we flew adjacent to a small village, we suddenly dropped back down to 200ft with the change in air conditions. It was a terrifying experience that was repeated several times on that flight.

We continued to maintain low altitude, flying over the barren waste of desert, but the turbulence we experienced was formidable.

As we had encountered before in other countries, there were two airports at Amman and our outdated topographical maps did not differentiate the military from the civil airports. However, we were becoming experts at recognising which was which and, as we approached Amman, we identified the correct airport before air traffic control gave us a QDM (the magnetic heading to the airfield).

By the time we were on our final approach to land, it was late in the afternoon and the temperature of the runway was considerably cooler than earlier in the day. George did not think to compensate for the lack of updraught, with the result that about 3ft off the tarmac Charlie Golf dropped like a stone. The aircraft bounced twice and then did a ground loop before coming to a halt.

Apart from acute embarrassment, neither George nor I were worse for wear and, amazingly, Charlie Golf did not sustain any damage.

We taxied to our parking bay and while George managed the necessary customs and immigration clearance, I oversaw the refuelling procedure.

George hadn't been gone long when I was surrounded by several members of the Royal Aero Club of Jordan and a couple of the ground engineers. It felt good to be among friendly faces again and, when George returned, we were able to joke with them about our less than graceful arrival in Amman.

It was during this banter that one of the ground engineers, Ramsey Matalka, told us he had gained his qualifications in Perth, Scotland, and that he had recognised G-ASCG as an aircraft he had worked on during his training. The three of us were amazed at the coincidence. We immediately felt a sense of comradeship with Ramsey and gratefully accepted his offer to stay with him at his parents' home. Ramsey's home was simple but comfortable and we were made extremely welcome by his family. Ramsey had to return to work, but George and I were very much at ease spending time talking with Mr and Mrs Matalka before we retired to bed.

—

Sunday 14 July
Amman, Jordan

Our room and beds were very comfortable, but I still did not sleep well. I am sure it was due to the emotion and anxiety of the previous day's travels. I had also developed a head cold. Nevertheless, George and I ate a hearty breakfast of cold meats, eggs and Jordanian fruits. I then helped Mrs Matalka clear away and wash the dishes. The household chores completed,

Ramsey took George and me back to the airport to send a signal through to Jeddah in Saudi Arabia seeking permission to travel through their country by following the pipeline. Ramsey also wanted to inspect Charlie Golf. This took longer than expected, so there was no time for sightseeing before lunch. Even though it was one of the hottest days we had experienced so far, lunch turned out to be home-cooked chicken, potatoes and vegetables.

Mr and Mrs Matalka had to attend a relative's funeral in Madabah, so we all piled into the car for the enjoyable drive through some very impressive scenery. In Madabah, we were introduced to Ramsey's relatives while he busied himself making up refreshments to take with us on our sightseeing tour. That afternoon, Ramsey took us to a high point where we could look over the Jordan Valley and see the Dead Sea. We then stood in the place where Moses is thought to have stood when he first saw the Promised Land looking out over the Dead Sea, Jericho and Jerusalem.

Unfortunately, we were unable to see Jerusalem because of the heat haze and mist and, because of the war front, we were not able to get a closer vantage point. I found the vista breathtaking and was reminded of all the Bible stories I learned as a youngster in Sunday school. After drinking from a fresh-water well, Ramsey took us to an excavated building to show us the most astounding intricate and ancient mosaic. The whole afternoon George and I took heaps of photographs and movie film. While driving to yet another relative's house, Ramsey told us that while in Scotland he married a Scottish girl. Sadly, the marriage didn't work and his wife refused to return to Jordan with him and so he was waiting for his divorce to come through. Back with the whole family again, we all sat down to a traditional Jordanian meal of spiced meats and rice.

We returned to Amman, freshened up, then the three of

us headed off to a nightclub for a night out. We drank, danced and talked until after 1.00am. We left when an American, who lived adjacent to the club, started playing very loud music to drown out that being played in the nightclub. Once back at Matalka's place, we shared a few more drinks before all turning in for the night.

Monday 15 July
Amman, Jordan

Monday turned out to be the hottest and laziest day. By the time George and I breakfasted, Ramsey had already worked his shift for the day.

We badly needed clean clothes, so I joined Mrs Matalka on the roof of the house overlooking the streets of Amman. There we washed our clothes in tubs before hanging them out on a rope line. A rather primitive domestic experience indeed, but it did get the clothes clean. Back in the house, I was starting to feel sick with the heat, but did find enough energy to write a few letters home. In the late afternoon, George, Ramsey and I went back to the airport to find out if we had a response from our signal to Jeddah, only to be told that nothing had come through for us as yet. We then called in to the Royal Aero Club of Jordan to see if we could get a more recent map of the region. A very rude and snobbish aero club official refused to help us and told us that we had to come back the next morning.

While we were gone from the house, the decision had been made to drive up to Ramsey's uncle's house in the mountains for some relief from the heat. So, armed with plenty of sandwiches and drinks, the whole family piled into the car. It was dark when we got there, but we had a wonderful evening sitting under the stars in the cool, evening breeze surrounded by sweet-smelling pine trees. We were told that the King of Jordan's palace was just a few blocks away. I fell asleep in the car on the way back to Amman.

That night, possibly because I had allowed myself to relax, I realised I was losing my nerve. I was overwhelmed with fear and apprehension of having to fly again and I was becoming increasingly concerned about the alcohol we consumed in our spare time. My husband always had a bottle of whisky available for just one more drink.

—

Tuesday 16 July
Amman, Jordan

George got out of bed first that morning and at 6.00am he and Ramsey went to the airport to see if we had received a reply to our signal, seeking permission to fly into Saudi Arabia. An hour later, I received a call from him telling me to quickly pack our gear and get to the airport as soon as possible. I bade farewell to Mr and Mrs Matalka and in a sheer state of nerves hired a taxi to take me to the airport.

The next few hours were spent in utter hectic confusion trying to organise an acceptable flight plan across Saudi Arabia that would keep us on a safe and achievable route to Australia. The captain of the Aero Club was very supportive and he tried his damndest to persuade the officials to permit Charlie Golf to fly a shorter route than was demanded of us, but to no avail. The aviation authorities wouldn't compromise.

This is where we broke the rules. We plotted a route that was well within our fuel range, but would take us between two danger zones. We then filed a flight plan different from our plotted route. The official flight plan scheduled us to leave at 05.00 and showed our route as via Aqaba. This distance was well beyond our capabilities, but air traffic control did not necessarily know this and they certainly didn't question it. There is no doubt we were taking a huge risk. Once again it was either that, or pack up and go back home to Scotland.

I think the captain of the Aero Club must have understood our dilemma, or perhaps he just felt sorry for us. Whatever the reason, he took us to a very high-class restaurant in Amman and treated us to a slap-up meal on his expense account.

While at the Aero Club, we met and talked at length with yet another most interesting character. This time it was a young sheikh, aged about 25, and dressed in an expensive Western-style suit, who was taking flying lessons. We learned that he was a multi-millionaire who owned an aircraft company and had dozens of cars. My diary notes do not record his name.

Ramsey caught up with us after our meal and we returned to his home for our last night in Jordan. The Matalkas' hospitality seemed endless. Because of the stifling heat, we all returned to the uncle's house in the mountains where we spent a second evening enjoying the cool air under the pine trees while nibbling on Jordanian delicacies and, of course, drinking.

Perhaps it was the relaxing time spent in the mountain retreat, but on the way back down to Amman that evening I realised my confidence was returning and my fear of flying again in Charlie Golf was much less intense.

Chapter 11

Saudi Arabia

Searing heat and American hospitality

Wednesday 17 July 1968

Amman – Badanah, Saudi Arabia

Time of departure: 03.15 GMT Flying time: 3hrs.59mins

Flying conditions: Hot, visibility reasonable. Wind direction and velocity: 310°/15knots.

After three days and four nights in the care of a generous and most hospitable family, we sadly left Amman at 5.15am local time.

Our flight to Badanah, an American compound on the Saudi Arabian pipeline, was a navigator's dream. All my landmarks came into view as expected and we were "spot on" schedule, but it was still so very hot. Coming from the cooler climate of Scotland, the heat was the one continuous aggravation we had trouble coping with.

Despite this, George executed a perfect landing on the gravel strip of Badanah and we taxied over to the fuelling shed. Seeing there was no one available, I stayed with Charlie Golf while George went for a walk to find someone. I sweltered in that heat with no shelter for over thirty minutes before George returned in a car driven by Mr Jason, the American who managed the compound/base. Mr Jason then took us to the administration centre and, leaving George to manage the necessary paperwork, drove me across the base to the guest house. We were invited to stay overnight. How could I refuse such an offer when the room was very comfortable, air-conditioned and came with free access to the contents of the ice box.

After a most welcome shower and freshening up, we returned to the main centre for a lunch of American cuisine: noodle soup, beans and frankfurters. As we were leaving the dining room, Mr Jason met us and told us we could enjoy the use of the base swimming pool if we felt like it. We met Mr Jason's daughters at the pool and, while we lazed in the sun, had our first introduction to iced tea — home made, with cold, infused tea from the teapot, ice and lemons. We also graciously accepted an invitation to have dinner with the Jasons at their home.

Later in the afternoon, after Charlie Golf was refuelled and the writing chores done, we made our way over to Mr Jason's house. We soon discovered that Mr Jason was quite a character. His home was quite luxurious and sported elephant-leg stools and about five stuffed African deer heads decorating the walls. He claimed he shot all the animals. We also noted how quickly his wife and daughters respectfully obeyed every time he gave an order or made a request. Dinner that night at the Jason's consisted of one huge BBQ steak (we could have had a second one if desired), roast potatoes and salads. After we had eaten, our host suggested we all go out to the airstrip where the family could have a look at Charlie Golf. We returned to our room en route the town of Ar Ar.

Considering the sights and scenery George and I had seen so far in our travels, we found Ar Ar to be nothing special. As we were saying our thanks and goodbyes outside our sleeping quarters, Mr Jason handed us a bag of goodies for our trip the following day. We opened it to find a box of salt pills, four chocolate Mars bars and four hundred cigarettes. I don't know how we were supposed to carry chocolate Mars bars with us in that heat, but his kindness was heart-warming.

It must be noted that to own, carry or consume alcohol in Saudi Arabia was a serious crime punishable by imprisonment and/or a public flogging. The pipeline compounds/bases, being American territory, were exempt from this law as long as alcohol was flown in directly and not taken beyond the perimeter fence. So, again, we were taking a dreadful risk as George still had two bottles of whisky in our luggage, one of which was already opened and the seal broken.

—

Thursday 18 July
Badanah — Qaisumah, Saudi Arabia
Time of departure: 03.42 GMT Flying time: 3hrs 34mins
Flying conditions: Extreme heat, poor visibility due to sand haze. Wind direction and velocity: north-east.

We were supposed to be up and ready for a 4.00am start, but we were both asleep when the driver knocked on the door. It didn't take us long to pull ourselves together and the driver didn't have to wait too long.

We had a great start to the day's flying. En-route to Qaisumah, we were blessed with a very strong tail wind and, much to our delight, we were bowling along at approximately ninety knots. Just as well, because this wind was so hot we had to travel with windows and vents closed. All we could do was to sit and swelter. Concentrating was difficult and we were both feeling somewhat cranky and out-of-sorts. Having to fly and navigate through the dense sand haze didn't help. Despite this, we arrived at Qaisumah on time and Charlie Golf touched down beautifully on the air strip.

As I got down out of the aircraft, my legs buckled and I felt very weak. I seemed to have lost my strength and energy. After the gruelling task of refuelling Charlie Golf in the searing hot wind and relentless sun, the Pumping Station Superintendent, Mr Babbs, took pity on us and drove us to the base dining room where we consumed much needed drinks of iced water. Once again, we were allowed to rest up in the guest house. This accommodation was just as welcome and comfortable as that in Badanah. I downed a couple of salt pills, then dropped onto the bed and slept for two or three hours in the cool air. Feeling only slightly better, I managed to wash out some clothes before Mr Babbs returned at 5.00pm to take us to his house for pre-dinner drinks. I downed another couple of salt tablets and began to feel much revived.

Once again we enjoyed the hospitality of our host as we wined, dined and chatted with his family in the main dining room. We decided an early night was in order, but we still found time to pack all our gear and prepare for the next day's flight before turning in.

—

Friday 19 July
Qaisumah — Ras Tanura, Saudi Arabia

Time of departure: 02.07 GMT Flying time: 4hrs 32mins
Flying conditions: Humid with strong head winds. Wind direction and velocity: n/a.

We had been travelling for exactly one month and that morning we did not have any difficulty with a 3.00am start. The early night in bed had paid off. We just had time to grab a cup of coffee before Mr Babbs arrived to take us to the airstrip.

Amazingly, there was no wind. As we climbed aboard Charlie Golf, Mr Babbs handed us a food parcel that Mrs Babbs had thoughtfully made up for us. Once airborne and on track, we tucked into a welcome breakfast of hard boiled eggs and sandwiches.

We were still following the pipeline, but what we didn't realise was that we were flying against a very strong head wind. Of course, there were no accurate Met reports available to us on this section of the trip. We had to rely solely on the knowledge and experience of the men who managed the airstrips and our own observations. So, after four hours flying time, we were still flying the pipeline, but I could not get an accurate bearing on our position. We calculated that we had to be close enough to the coast to enable us to pick up our bearings from there. Although risky, George turned Charlie Golf away from the pipeline and on to an easterly course. Sure enough, in a very short time, we had a coastline beneath us to assist in plotting our position.

The problem was we were still too far away from Dhahran to get there with our remaining fuel supply. Fortunately, our topographical map indicated there was an oil refinery with a useable airstrip approximately 25nautical miles north of our intended destination. We decided the safest strategy would be to land on the airstrip and beg some avgas. Despite a very strong direct crosswind at ground level, George brought Charlie Golf down perfectly.

As soon as we disembarked, we felt a difference in the heat. The searing dry heat of the desert had changed to being the clammy and humid heat of the coast.

Once again, George left me with Charlie Golf while he trekked the long walk from the airstrip to the oil refinery. He returned about an hour later with an entourage of Arab Government officials and company officers. We learned that our unscheduled landing was on an airstrip called Ras Tanura and our unexpected arrival had all the airstrip personnel running backwards and forwards in a flap. When things quietened down, the oil company representative took us back to his home where we were able to freshen up. We were also given refreshments of sandwiches, potato chips and Cokes. While our host contacted the Dhahran air traffic controllers, another officer was trying to locate somewhere for George and me to spend the night in Ras Tanura. I was taken to a guest house, while George returned to the airstrip to refuel Charlie Golf with high octane car fuel. Apparently, there was no aircraft refuelling facilities at Ras Tanura, so we had to compromise with ordinary petrol, filtered, of course.

—

Ras Tanura — Dhahran, Saudi Arabia

Time of departure: 14.14 GMT Flying time: 0.31mins
Flying Conditions: Cool and humid. Wind direction and velocity: n/a.

After a couple of hours' rest, we were taken back to the airstrip where we took off for a thirty-minute flight into Dhahran. Thankfully, Charlie Golf performed brilliantly on the substituted fuel.

As we taxied to a parking bay in Dhahran Airport we fully expected the full weight of the aviation authorities to come down on us from a great height. We held our breath waiting for the order to come over the radio to report to air traffic control immediately.

Amazingly, no one was the least bit interested in us, so much so that it took two hours to get someone to refuel Charlie Golf with avgas.

Dhahran Airport was one of the most exotic we'd encountered since Marseille. The terminal buildings looked like palaces; and it was very humid. One of the refuelling crew gave us a lift to the Airport Hotel and, despite the exorbitant cost, we decided to book in and eat in the dining room before going to bed. We were both exhausted.

Chapter 12

Qatar and Trucial States

Strong head winds and change of flight plan

Saturday 20 July 1968
Dhahran – Doha, Qatar
Time of departure: 02.37 GMT Flying time: 1hr 38mins
Flying conditions: Humid with heavy mist. Wind direction and velocity: n/a.

With great difficulty we both forced ourselves awake when the alarm clock rang out at 3.00am. As we were too early for breakfast at the hotel, we ordered a coffee instead and that had to suffice as breakfast. In the damp, humid dawn we made our way back to the airport, loaded up Charlie Golf then taxied out onto the runway. Because of the excessive dampness in the air Charlie Golf had developed a magneto drop, but after about ten minutes George got us rolling forward for take-off.

We had intended to fly direct to Abu Dhabi from Dhahran, but not long into our flight we realised we were once more battling a strong head-wind and it would take us much longer to get there than we had first calculated. We were still very weary through lack of sleep, so rather than push our luck and take risks we could easily avoid, we decided to cut this trip short and land at Doha, Qatar. We had no problem changing our flight plan and we received a very good reception from the aviation officials and the air traffic controllers at Doha. This seemed a good sign, so we decided to give up any thoughts of more flying on that day and to stay overnight. The weather was still very warm and the humidity extremely high.

Because we now had time to spare, we got chatting with the air traffic controllers only to learn that one, we can only recall as Ian, was a very good friend of Whin Watkins, our good host in Tripoli. To add to this, Ian was also considering flying a single-engine Auster to Australia. After we made sure Charlie Golf was secure and we cleared customs, we left the airport with Ian as he had kindly invited us to stay the night with him, his wife and two children.

Once again, we ate a delicious, hot meal in the middle of the day. After filling up on chicken with all the trimmings, George decided he was too tired to go sightseeing in the town and so the two of us went to bed at 4.00pm and slept very sound until the next morning.

—

Sunday 21 July

Doha — Sharjah, Trucial States (United Arab Emirates)

Time of departure: 02.08 GMT Flying time: 3hrs 42mins
Flying conditions: Hot, less humid, changeable wind Wind direction and velocity: n/a.

We must have been exhausted, as we slept sound for twelve hours. On waking, we found that Ian's wife had left a note asking us to awaken her. She made us coffee, then gave us the keys for their mini car to drive ourselves to the airport. Even though it was early morning and not as hot and humid as the previous day, we still perspired profusely.

Our original flight plan indicated a stop and refuel at Abu Dhabi. However, the flying conditions and the visibility that day were the best we had experienced for a while, so we overflew

Abu Dhabi and continued on to the RAF base at Sharjah. Despite the strong crosswinds on the runway allocated to us, George executed yet another perfect landing.

As it was Sunday, movement on the base was slow and so we had to wait for a while in the control tower before we were allocated hangar space and before we could refuel Charlie Golf.

The introduction letter given to us by Colonel De Butt in Cairo was addressed to a Major Budd. Being Sunday, however, Major Budd was apparently at the beach, so his acting officer took us to sleeping quarters to enable us to change, freshen up and have several cold beers.

Back at the control tower, George spent time talking with the controllers while I went with our host to the dining room to try out their curry.

The air traffic controllers tried to arrange for us to stay in accommodation on the base, but the more senior controller wouldn't allow it, so we had to wait until contact was made with the RAF. At 6.30pm, arrangements were finally made for us to stay at yet another controller's flat in Dubai.

While waiting for our newly appointed host, George and I went to the dining room for an enjoyable tea of omelette and chips. We were back in the sleeping quarters that we had been allocated when suddenly the door burst open and three very boisterous blokes barged in carrying a crate of beer. Peter Lennan introduced himself as our host, stating that it was OK to stay at his pad because his wife had gone back to the U.K. for ten days.

More drinking and talking ensued until the beer was finished and we were all rather drunk. Then Peter, George and I piled into Peter's Mini Moke and headed for his pad. The Mini Moke seemed the perfect vehicle for getting around Dubai. We were greatly impressed with Peter's accommodation. It was very luxurious and we felt privileged to be invited to stay.

Peter made coffee for us all and then I headed for bed while he and George continued with the alcohol and talk.

—

Monday 22 July
Sharjah, Trucial States

The bed in Peter's flat was huge and very comfortable. Unfortunately, probably due to the combination of curry and alcohol, I was up at least four times in the night, so I didn't get the best night's sleep. At 7.00am local time, Peter spoiled us by giving us a cup of tea in bed. It was quite a luxury. After a bacon sandwich for breakfast, the three of returned to the RAF base.

The RAF ground engineers had taken us under their wing and decided that Charlie Golf needed a thorough inspection before we continued our travels to Australia. The engineer who had worked on Austers in the past gave Charlie Golf a good "going over" and reported that the only things needing attention were arrester wires that had frayed and needed to be bound. After he had finished the overhaul and repairs, the engineer stuck their mascot of a black cat on the port side fuselage of Charlie Golf. We also asked to have the compass serviced because at times the needle would stick and it would require a hefty thump to get it swinging again.

The transfer of the cat on the cowling can be seen on subsequent photos taken of us with the aircraft. I also noticed in those photographs that we both appear to have lost weight, being considerably thinner than when we first left Scotland.

George and I had lunch and drinks in the officers' mess and then went back to Peter's to catch up on washing and other overdue chores. Dinner that night was sausage and beans and then it was back to the officers' mess for more drinking and socialising with the No 78 Squadron. We recalled so many incidents and answered that many questions relating to our trip that we were getting sick of the sound of our own voices. Notwithstanding, it was flattering and heart-warming to receive so much interest and attention.

Again, under the influence of too much alcohol, we returned with Peter to his flat and fell into bed.

—

Tuesday 23 July
Sharjah, Trucial States

Another day spent in Sharjah. As Peter was on duty in the tower, we were invited to join the No 78 Squadron as they celebrated the departure of one of their own who was heading back to the U.K. to get married. In the afternoon, we recorded a radio interview at Sharjah radio studios to be played over the force's radio station.

We were planning to continue our travels the following morning, so George stocked up at the NAAFI (Navy, Army and Air Force Institute) with four bottles of whisky and six hundred cigarettes. That night we cooked and fended for ourselves as Peter was going out for the evening. This gave me the opportunity to catch up on the diary writing and to get our gear ready before going to bed.

—

Wednesday 24 July
Sharjah, Trucial States

We were now five weeks into our trip and starting to get concerned about the approaching monsoons. Our long-term plan was to be well ahead of the monsoon season as we travelled through the Pakistan, India and Burma regions. Because of the delays we had experienced to date, the monsoon season was looming too close for comfort and we needed to be on our way again.

Much to our frustration, the Met report indicated strong head winds on our route to Jiwani, Pakistan. So strong, in fact, we could not possibly reach Jiwani with Charlie Golf's limited fuel range. Refuelling in Iran was absolutely out of the question. We had to fly direct to Pakistan. The only alternative was to refuel at Dibba, an airstrip on the other side of the peninsular from Dubai. However, we were informed that there was no fuel or facilities available. The good news was that helicopter exercises were being conducted by the RAF in that region and the pilots were prepared to drop off two jerry cans of avgas at Dibba for our use the following day.

We were extremely grateful for the effort these guys made to enable us to continue our travels. We were shown the utmost courtesy and showered with hospitality that was well beyond our expectations. So it was with embarrassment that we accepted yet another offer of accommodation in the sleeping quarters at Sharjah, even if we were separated — George in the male quarters and me in the female.

That evening in the officers' mess, after more drinking and dinner, we watched the movie *Funeral in Berlin* starring Michael Caine.

—

Thursday 25 July

Sharjah — Dibba — Sharjah, Trucial States

Time of departure: 01.58 GMT Flying time: 2hrs 09mins
Flying conditions: Cloud over Dibba Wind direction & velocity: n/a.

George collected me from my sleeping quarters at 5.00am local time, as arranged. We checked the Met report for the day, paid our landing fees, and filed a flight plan as required. So far all things were going well and to plan. A few of our ground crew acquaintances waved us farewell as we lifted off the runway and set course for Dibba. It didn't take long to reach our refuelling stop. However, as we approached, we were faced with an early morning cloud layer that rose to approximately 3,500ft and stretched from the nearby mountains as far as we could see out over the sea. The sun had started to burn some of the cloud off, but after circling nearby for approximately forty-five minutes, we still didn't have enough visibility to put down. Even if we could land at this point, we had used up more fuel in circling and those few jerry cans of top-up fuel on the ground at Dibba would still not give us enough range to get into Pakistan. As such, we returned to Sharjah.

Perhaps this was fortunate because a quick check of Charlie Golf after we landed revealed that the inspection Perspex for the starboard wing fuel tank was missing. This could have been disastrous if the surrounding canvas had started to rip in flight. George effected a satisfactory repair of the wing in the hangar while I, rather sheepishly, called on the good nature of the RAF and arranged for yet another night's accommodation and hospitality at the base.

We laid low the rest of that day and for four hours in the afternoon we caught up on some much needed sleep. The evening was spent in the officer's mess with dinner, drinks and more socialising before heading back to bed.

—

Friday 26 July

Sharjah – Dibba, Trucial States

Time of departure: 03.33 GMT Flying time: 0.53mins

Flying conditions: Humid, cooler with some cloud Wind direction and velocity: n/a.

That morning, we decided to delay time of departure to give any possible cloud cover over Dibba time to burn off. We also decided to travel with a maximum fuel load so we once again took off with the plastic container full of avgas on my knee.

This time we managed to fly under the cloud and follow a *wadi* (Arabic name for a dry river bed) to the army camp. We circled the army camp as instructed, then flew back to the airstrip at Dibba. After a first class landing on the strip, we were joined by a Jeep full of soldiers from the camp. We refuelled Charlie Golf's belly tank with fuel provided by the military and then before taking off we proceeded to set up our in-flight fuelling system — that is, fitting the hose into the belly tank and up into the cockpit and wiring the aircraft door closed. I still had the container of avgas on my knee. I'm sure those observing us must have thought we were crazy. We probably were, but it was the only way we could keep going. Turning back was now absolutely out of the question.

Chapter 13

Pakistan

Friday 26 July 1968
Dibba – Jiwani, Pakistan
Time of departure: 05.12 GMT Flying time: 4hrs 34mins
Flying conditions: Visibility poor Wind direction and velocity: 200°/15knots.

Dibba to Jiwani was relatively incident-free and the mid-flight fuelling procedure worked like a charm. We were obviously becoming more experienced and gaining confidence and so this trip, although longer than the last few, was quite pleasant. Also, the cloud cover gave us relief from the heat and we enjoyed the cooler conditions.

On arrival at the Shell facilities of Jiwani, we were met by an extremely friendly local Pakistani ground crew. As had happened so many times before on our travels, the manager of this airstrip and surrounding facilities offered to put us up for the night as there was no other accommodation available in Jiwani.

Leaving the Middle East and entering Pakistan was another important benchmark in our travels from a psychological as well as physical perspective. Our experiences were also markedly different to those in the Middle East. However, by this time, I think George and I were prepared for almost any eventuality.

This being the case, it was really no surprise to find ourselves, with baggage in tow, piled onto the back of an old tractor with a few other ground crew and weaving our way across dusty terrain to the manager's bungalow.

The bungalow was a wooden shack with three small rooms and a veranda. Our accommodation for the night consisted of two iron beds, each with a mattress, one small table, thousands of flies and millions of ants. We considered ourselves to be quite fortunate as the only alternative was to sleep on the airstrip.

We discovered that Jiwani was an ex World War II airstrip maintained by Karachi Aviation with one scheduled passenger flight per week to service the local needs.

As it was still early in the day, our host took us for a sightseeing drive along the coast in his Jeep. The gravel beaches were littered with many local fishing vessels, all in different stages of repair and maintenance. He also took us to a "dead" town that was once the hub for the BOAC flying boats that landed on the water-filled creek. We found the history of this small corner of the Arabian Sea quite fascinating.

More airstrip officials, all men, were waiting for us when we returned to the bungalow. Another hour or so of questions and answers ensued. We really didn't mind, and found the attention reassuring. When they took their leave, we were ushered into another room for a dinner of very hot curry and rice. The curry was too hot for me, but George enjoyed it. I didn't know what the base meat of the curry was.

That night we slept in our jeans and shirts and with the doors and shutters open.

Interestingly, my diary notes do not indicate the presence of women. I believe this was probably due to the fact we were flying a light aircraft that, by its very nature, was a male-oriented activity that attracted the interests of the men. Women seemed to be on the peripheral of our socialising, though I have no doubt they would have cooked the meals and prepared our accommodation.

—

Saturday 27 July
Jiwani — Karachi, Pakistan

Time of departure: 04.29 GMT Flying time: 4hrs 01min
Flying conditions: Cool, low cloud, sea fog Wind direction and velocity: 230°/15knots.

We woke as dawn broke, although neither George nor I slept very well. We quickly gave ourselves a "camp" wash, then enjoyed a breakfast of two fried eggs each, provided and prepared by our host family. After breakfast, we were ferried to the airstrip in the Jeep by the manager. Having completed all the necessary administrative tasks, we left Jiwani, once again with the belly tank hose securely in place and the container of avgas in the cockpit to ensure Charlie Golf made the distance.

As we followed the coast part of the way, the sea mist was quite severe. However, navigation was easy and, in general, it was a pleasant flight. As we made radio contact with Karachi air traffic control, we were pleased to be given a "radar" approach without requesting one. This certainly made our task easier, especially given Karachi had a great deal of international commercial traffic. Unfortunately, our landing was not the most professional, as Charlie Golf bounced several times with the tail swinging from side to side.

We parked Charlie Golf as instructed and, as was our usual routine, we refuelled before making our way to sort out the customs and immigration requirements. On the way we stopped at the bar for a drink and when George was charged £0.17s for one beer, we decided to call it quits at one.

First, we attempted to clear customs. Whether it was because we had flown internally from Jiwani, or whether it was because we were piloting our own private, single-engine aircraft, we will never really know, but the officials on duty had absolutely no idea what to do with us, with the result that we, with all our baggage in tow, were shunted backwards and forwards all over the airport from one customs officer to another. Eventually, we were so angry and frustrated, and no doubt tired, that not only were we shouting abuse at the officials but we were losing our tempers with each other. Finally, we were given customs and immigration clearance.

Then, when we hailed a taxi and were about to get in, we noticed that the taxi meter was already registering what seemed to be a high fare. Another argument ensued and tempers frayed before the taxi driver brought the meter back to an acceptable flag-fall and we headed into the city of Karachi. So I guess it was no surprise when we discovered the cost of the medium rate hotel was extortionate for our standards and tight budget.

As if things weren't bad enough, as part of the book-in procedure, the hotel receptionist asked us for extremely inappropriate personal information that we considered to be totally irrelevant.

With George and I still at loggerheads when we got up to our room, I decided I would take out my anger and frustration on some washing. Unfortunately, in my annoyance, I accidently kicked over a precious bottle of whisky that was beside the baggage behind the door. Because of the hard terrazzo floor, of course the bottle smashed and the contents flowed out across the room. George, thinking I had smashed it on purpose, was absolutely furious. I had never seen him so angry before and I was so terrified I shut myself in the toilet and locked the door. I stayed there while George arranged for the hotel porters to pick up the glass and mop up the whisky.

By the time the mess was cleaned up George's anger had cooled, despite the fact he had only one bottle of duty-free whisky left. While locked in the bathroom, I took the opportunity to calm myself down by taking a shower.

When the atmosphere was considerably calmer, I emerged and, feeling very lonely and homesick, quietly assumed writing the diary and catching up with letters to send home.

The unpleasant, heavy atmosphere was partially broken when the porter arrived with chicken sandwiches and coffee. However, we maintained a cold aloofness when we later went down to dinner in the hotel dining room.

During the meal, George was called out to the reception desk to take a telephone call. The call was from a reporter of the *Karachi Evening Star* requesting to interview us at the hotel. We had just finished our meal when two reporters arrived. We were becoming experts at anticipating questions and giving factual information that seemed to excite and satisfy the curiosity of others. The photographer took our photo and George gave them one of Charlie Golf to take with them on condition that it was returned to us.

By bedtime, we were both utterly emotionally, psychologically and physically exhausted. However, the interlude with the reporters had made us forget our animosity towards each other and we were back on reasonably civil speaking terms.

The return of media interest, after having none for weeks, made us think that perhaps other people were starting to believe that we might possibly make it all the way to Australia. It somehow gave us confidence and boosted our morale, although, as I dropped off to sleep that night, I distinctly remember thinking I couldn't possibly cope with another day like that.

—

Sunday 28 July
Karachi, Pakistan

There was no air conditioning in our hotel room and, with the weather so hot and humid, we found it difficult to sleep comfortably. This morning we decided to take a taxi to downtown Karachi to sightsee in the markets and bazaars and to take photographs. We were very much reminded of the squalor of Cairo. The streets were filthy, food and merchandise stalls were sprawled along the sidewalks, and beggars were abundant, in particular, very young children in the arms of their mothers, disabled and maimed men and women, and groups of dirty, young children laughing and shouting as they followed us.

We were now so used to these surroundings that we could virtually ignore the bustle around us and concentrate on shopping for our immediate needs. George bought a pair of sandals and, with great difficulty, we eventually found a small store that sold postcards, so I bought a dozen to ensure we always had a supply.

Back at the hotel, we showered to freshen up and get rid of the street grime. After lunch, we went back out to Karachi Airport to order a Met report and to file a flight plan for the following day.

In 1968, Pakistan, India, and the then East Pakistan (now Bangladesh), had broken off all diplomatic relations with each other and were virtually in a state of "cold war". As we were to soon discover, this did not go well for us.

We were informed that Jamnagar, our next scheduled stop in India, was in fact an Indian Air Force base protecting the border between the two countries, and so out of bounds to private aircraft, that is, unless we had written permission from the Indian director general of the civil aviation and military authorities in Delhi.

George and I, being small fry, had Buckley's chance of working our way through that administrative nightmare. We reasoned our best shot was to seek out the British Embassy in Karachi and ask the Attaché to contact his counterpart in the British Embassy in Delhi. Hopefully, the Attaché in Delhi could speed up the paperwork and seek the required permission on our behalf, given we were on a very fine timeline to keep in front of the monsoons.

Next step was to locate the British Embassy in the local telephone directory. In the telephone listings we found the name of Squadron Leader Howard, Assistant Air Adviser to the High Commission. We noted the squadron leader's address, then hailed a taxi. Being a Sunday, we reasoned he would most likely be at home and not at the offices of the High Commission.

This was easier said than done. The taxi driver, George and I had dreadful trouble locating the address given in the directory. After seeking directions from the locals at least four times, the taxi driver finally found the house, only to be told that Mr Howard had moved house a short while ago. It was another one of those days.

By this time, we were very hot and frustrated, so we implemented plan B. The taxi driver took us to a decent snack bar where the staff were extremely helpful and understanding. As we cooled down with much needed drinks, the proprietor kindly made all the necessary calls in his native tongue and was soon able to give us the correct telephone number and address. Using the same taxi driver, we immediately made our way to Squadron Leader Howard's residence.

Much to our relief, Squadron Leader Stanford Howard was in residence, and we soon discovered that he and his wife,

Judy, were extremely pleasant, helpful and empathetic to our plight. Squadron Leader Howard promised to get the paperwork moving as a priority the first thing on Monday morning. For several hours we sat talking and drinking with the Howards until at about 9.00pm when we took a taxi back to our hotel. By this time, the alcohol and probably the temporary respite from our problem were taking effect and the diary notes indicate *we engaged in great hilarity during our evening meal at the hotel then fell into bed.*

Monday 29 July
Karachi, Pakistan

It was so humid during the night that I had to get up at 3.00am and stand under a cold shower before I could get any sleep. During breakfast, we were pleasantly surprised when the hotel porter brought us the photograph that George had lent the reporters. Being rather cynical, we assumed we had seen the last of it. Later that morning, George contacted Stanford only to learn that a response from India was not yet forthcoming. However, the squadron leader instructed George and me to vacate the hotel and make our way to the offices of the British High Commission. We packed our gear, vacated our room, but left our luggage in the hotel foyer while we had lunch.

Before paying our bill, George had arranged for a bearer (hotel porter) to purchase some Paludrine anti-malaria tablets for us. He was gone for over an hour, and when he returned demanded over £0.12s from us for taxi fares. My diary notes do not indicate how this latest disagreement over money was resolved, but I am certain the bearer did not get the full amount of his demands.

We were later than expected arriving at the British High

Commission, but it made no difference, we still hadn't received a response to our request. We learned, however, that Stanford and Judy Howard were more than happy to offer us accommodation in the luxurious apartment in the upstairs section of their home. Once ensconced in our new surroundings, we made ourselves presentable, then joined Stanford, Judy and their baby son in the lounge room for pre-dinner drinks. We dined at 9.00pm on soup, chicken and chips and continued socialising with our new-found friends until bedtime.

—

Tuesday 30 July
Karachi, Pakistan

That morning, we were woken by a servant bringing us a cup of coffee. George got up immediately and went with Stanford to the High Commission building to await a reply from Delhi. I dozed 'til about 10.30am, when Judy came into our room with baby Stanford and we sat on the bed and nattered. She left to enable me to dress and then I joined her later in her room where she was busy sewing. Our washing had been given to the *Dobi* to do, so I was relieved of my chores. I think both Judy and I had been yearning for and welcomed the company of like-minded females because we talked 'til George and Stanford returned for lunch. Still no word from Delhi was forthcoming. However, Stanford told us we had all been invited out to lunch the following day with the Beagle Terrier aircraft agent in Karachi, apparently a very wealthy gentleman.

After lunch at the Howard's home, Stanford dropped Judy, the baby and me at the Sind Club swimming pool for an afternoon of pure, cool relaxation. George stayed behind to catch up on sleep. We returned to the house at 5.00pm and, as Judy and Stanford were going out for the evening, George and I were left to our own devices, so we consumed a few more drinks, then dined alone on a delicious beef curry prepared by the in-house cook. The diary notes indicate that we were once again slightly under the influence of alcohol when we went to bed.

—

Wednesday 31 July
Karachi, Pakistan

Wednesday morning was spent in the Howards' living room discussing the religious rituals of the Pakistani people. Judy told us of the sacrifice of a young child at a religious festival held the year before not far from their previous home in Karachi.

As we were getting ready to go to lunch, Stanford returned with the news that it would be at least another forty-eight hours before we could expect a response from India. We were bitterly disappointed, but that was quickly pushed to the back of our minds when we arrived at the luncheon venue.

We were delightfully surprised and very flattered to learn that the luncheon was being held in our honour. There were fourteen other invited guests from the aviation community and down the centre of the table was the word WELCOME in fresh green leaves. Needless to say, the afternoon was spent eating, drinking and discussing the details of our aircraft and the adventures of our journey so far.

After a late afternoon nap, we found ourselves socialising again with Stanford and Judy in their living room. Later in the evening, we all agreed sausages, beans and chips would be a great supper.

We retired that evening, well fed, and relaxed after a most enjoyable day.

It was about this time during our stay with Stanford and Judy that we began to sense there was more to Stanford's role with the

British Consulate than appeared on the surface. We recall, for example, that on at least one occasion in the late afternoon when we were out in the car with him driving, he stopped on or beside the bridge that went over the main passenger and freight railway lines that went into Karachi. He then produced a pair of compact, high-strength binoculars and proceeded to closely examine the passing rail traffic. He made light of his activity, saying that he just liked to keep up with the latest comings and goings of the local trade, but, as I recall, he particularly requested that we didn't make mention of it in our diary or speak of it with others.

At a much later date, we also wondered if our room had been bugged. Two issues raised this concern.

The first thing that happened was when I was with Judy. She appeared obsessed with a specific brand of expensive china and tableware and, as she was about to send overseas for an order, she tried to persuade me to order some. For George and I, this brand of crockery was well out of our price range and at that time we could not afford such luxuries. I recall talking to George about it when we were in our room that evening and it was after that discussion that Judy's friendship cooled considerably and the chinaware was never mentioned again.

The second issue was that on top of our bedside tables, positioned in full view, was a fully illustrated edition of the *Kama Sutra* along with other mildly pornographic reading material. Neither George nor I had been exposed to anything quite so erotic or graphic before and, to be honest, it made us laugh.

Was our room bugged? We will never know ... In private, we jokingly spoke of James Bond and diplomatic spies, but at the time did not think too seriously about it.

Notwithstanding, we were still extremely grateful for the hospitality and hand of friendship they proffered.

—

Thursday 1 August
Karachi, Pakistan

Stanford and Judy had already left the house by the time we got up, so after a light breakfast of toast and coffee I caught up with the chores while George went out to the airport to check that all was well with Charlie Golf. After I finished my chores, I spent the rest of the morning playing with baby Stanford.

When Stanford Snr returned for lunch, we were relieved to learn there had been a response from India giving us permission to land in Bhuj. The bad news was that there was no guarantee that avgas fuel would be available at each one of our scheduled stops across India. Another signal had been sent to the High Commission in India for further clarification.

That afternoon, George and I shut ourselves in our room and busied ourselves with pre-flight planning for the next step of our journey.

As Judy and Stanford had another commitment for dinner that evening, George and I decided we would go into the city and spoil ourselves with a meal at the Hong Kong Chinese Restaurant in Karachi. As the evening wore on, and with things seemingly not going his way, George lost his temper and started forcefully arguing with the restaurant staff. I realised he probably had rather a lot to drink and felt it was becoming rather a worrying habit.

Hoping to retrieve some pleasure and romance in the evening, I agreed to go for a walk. George chose a route that took us through the dirtiest, dingiest streets of the *Souk*. Of course, once we left the main streets used by westerners and other tourists, we were once again surrounded and harassed by groups of young men trying to nudge and touch me. Although I was tired and repulsed by this sort of attention, I put up with it as I knew George loved the mystery and intrigue the back streets had to offer. However, I did not feel I could cope with yet another heated and emotional argument, but the inevitable happened and George ended up very loudly exchanging abuse with a local teenager. Immediately, we were surrounded by a mob of men all pushing forward to see and probably join the melee. We somehow managed to break away and jump into a taxi. By the time we got back to the Howards' home I was terrified and also angry at allowing ourselves to be caught in such circumstances again.

—

Friday 2 August
Karachi, Pakistan

I slept fitfully and was still angry and confused when it was time to get up. However, George apologised for his behaviour of the previous evening and, recognising the sentiment was sincere, I accepted.

During that morning, Stanford telephoned to say our route across India had been approved, so George returned to the airport to file a flight plan while I packed and prepared our gear for a much-awaited, early morning take-off to India.

We should have gone to bed early that night to get as much rest as we could, but instead we again spent the time socialising and enjoying Stanford's tales of his experiences in the medical corps.

Chapter 14

India — Western Border

Under close guard and an apparition

Saturday 3 August 1968
Karachi — Bhuj, India
Time of departure: 05.53 GMT Flying time: 2hrs 20mins
Flying conditions: Poor visibility, no landmarks for tracking.
Wind direction and velocity: 250°/20knots.

I woke at 6.00am with stomach problems, probably due to the revelling of the previous evening. I woke George and we breakfasted on boiled eggs. After taking lots of photographs and promising to keep in touch we finally bade farewell to our hosts of the past week.

It was 7.15am when we reached the airport and, much to our dismay, we received exactly the same "pass the buck" treatment as when we first arrived in Karachi. Nobody seemed to know how to process our flight plan, landing fees and exit fees. Quite a debacle ensued until finally we were cleared to take off at 10.53am, local time.

Unfortunately, because of the humidity and dense mist, the visibility was extremely poor. To make navigation even more difficult, we were flying over bare, flat terrain with precious few landmarks to give us an accurate bearing. Approximately one hour into our flight, our radio transmitter picked up Bombay IFR (Instrument Flight Rules control) calling Golf Alpha Sierra

Charlie Golf. George responded with, 'Golf Alpha Sierra Charlie Golf calling Bombay IFR, receiving you loud and clear; please go ahead'. After repeating this procedure several times, it was evident that we were receiving Bombay IFR reasonably clearly, but Bombay IFR could not hear us.

After a short pause, we heard, 'Golf Alpha Sierra Charlie Golf you are not, repeat not cleared to land in Bhuj. You are instructed to return to Pakistan'.

We couldn't believe it. We were led to believe that Stanford had received permission on our behalf to enter Indian air space.

Still unable to make radio contact with Bombay, George turned Charlie Golf back onto a heading for Karachi. We had been flying for about ten minutes bemoaning our misfortune and trying to quickly work out our next strategy when, unanimously, we decided "bugger it", we would have a much better chance of arguing our case for permission to cross India from within India than we would from neighbouring Pakistan.

So we turned around and once more set a compass course for Bhuj.

All these unplanned manoeuvres played absolute havoc with the accuracy of my navigating skills. We knew we were flying into Bhuj air space, but other than that I was quite flummoxed. Consequently, as soon as we had radio contact with Bhuj air traffic control, George asked for a QDM and soon located the airfield. Because of the 25-knot crosswind, our landing was rather bumpy, but we were down safe, and thankful we hadn't been shot at.

As soon as Charlie Golf slowed to a halt, we were surrounded by officers in uniform, Charlie Golf was impounded and we were marched to the airport manager's office.

Once in the office, we were faced with what appeared to us to be police and military (army and air force), as well as the airport officials. We were bombarded with questions from all parties. The police, in particular, asked what we thought at the time to be quite stupid and irrelevant questions, such as; 'What is your brother's name and occupation? When did your father die and of what?'

This time, George kept his cool and very calmly and civilly answered each and every question. To help prove our identity, we produced the newspaper cuttings of our trip that we had collected on the way. This must have added weight to our claims because we were eventually set free, on condition that we did not leave Bhuj until clearance was received from the civil aviation authorities in Delhi. We were also told that there was no avgas suitable for Charlie Golf available in Bhuj and so we would have to resort to filling up on filtered high octane car petrol.

The airport officials and the military, seemingly having finished, then herded us into a Jeep and drove us to a "most modern hotel" in town. Our room in the "most modern hotel" had an earth-and-stone floor, canvas roof, a flimsy, wooden partition separating us from the next room, two iron beds with lumpy, stained, kapok mattresses, one sheet and one blanket. Squashed tight between the two single beds was a small side table. I recall there was also just enough room at the end of the beds for a small, fragile, wooden dresser. There was no glass or curtains over the tiny holes in the wall, just bars with external wooden shutters.

When George asked about changing money, he was told that it would not be possible until Monday morning at 11.00am. This being Saturday, we were facing yet more delays in our itinerary.

We ate a light tea of omelette and coffee, then with one of our acquaintances who seemed to have become attached to us, we went for a walk to see what Bhuj had to offer in the way of tourist attractions.

Our new guide, or was he a minder, took us to see some spectacular temples that were adorned both inside and out with the most beautiful colourful paintings. The temples' stonework was completely covered in magnificent art works. A cage inside one particular temple contained a seated ivory figurine with diamond studded eyes and lips. This figurine was surrounded by other ornaments and fineries. George and I were awestruck as we had never seen anything quite like this before. We took plenty of photographs for our collection.

When we returned to our room, we were served a very unappetising meal of rice and "stew". Unfortunately, we felt obliged to eat it as our room was full of "local guests" who seemed to scrutinise our every move with fascination. Eventually we found ourselves on our own and bedded down for the night. We must have been tired because it didn't take long for us to drop off to sleep, despite the male voices talking continually in the room behind the flimsy, wooden partition.

—

Sunday 4 August
Bhuj, India

We must have slept well because it was 9.00am local time when we woke. As we finished a breakfast of fried eggs, toast and jam, one of the young boys who was perpetually hanging around told George that he had to go to the manager's house and take a telephone message. Apparently, the civil aviation authorities wanted us to change our itinerary as there was no avgas available between Nagpur and Calcutta.

We decided to return to the airstrip and negotiate from there. So, after a quick wash in the basin full of cold water, we set out to walk. As it was, two of the young guys we had met the day before just happened to catch up with us on their scooters and offered us a ride to the airport on the pillion seats. We happily accepted and it was really good fun.

Once at the airport, George once again laboriously explained to the officials that Charlie Golf could fly quite adequately on high octane petrol. So yet another wire was sent through to Delhi. Interestingly, while at the airport, we were introduced to a young Indian girl who was a pilot and who showed a great interest in us, Charlie Golf and our travels.

Back in our allotted accommodation, we again found it difficult to consume our lunch. The fresh fruit was a welcome exception. We also couldn't surreptitiously dispose of the food as our boy was constantly close by. At about 5.30pm we decided to get some exercise and go for a walk. Lo and behold, we were met at the entrance by two of the males who had attached themselves to us the previous day, one of whom we recognised to be a police officer. They very kindly offered to accompany us around town for our personal wellbeing.

Naive as we were, it was beginning to dawn on us that we were, in fact, being chaperoned and were probably under some form of house arrest. With this in mind, we made an excuse to return to the room for our camera and while we were there we tied cotton threads in strategic places. We were becoming highly suspicious that someone had been in our room the last two occasions we had been away. We joked about having watched too many James Bond movies.

Our two so-called guides took us for tea, then down into the town square — rather like a village green — to walk around. It became quite overwhelming as we were followed by mobs of local Indians. Being a Sunday, they too were out walking, but clearly found our presence to be the afternoon's entertainment.

By the time we stopped to talk to the young men who that morning had given us pillion rides on their scooters, George and I estimated we were surrounded by about two or three hundred locals.

In the middle of the town park stood a splendid rotunda of Victorian architecture. Seated in the rotunda a uniformed brass band was belting out British marching tunes with gusto. No doubt this was a regular Sunday afternoon performance. As George and I drew close with our entourage, we caught the attention of the musicians. Gradually, the music grew slower until it eventually faded out to silence. The musicians, with mouths agape, watched us walk by. As we passed, one by one they took up their instruments and resumed playing the tune exactly where they had left off. By the time we got to the gate, the band had resumed their voluminous and enthusiastic playing. The whole episode must have looked like an extract from a Charlie Chaplin movie. We were told later that most of the residents of Bhuj had never seen blue-eyed and blond white people before.

We also had the privilege to visit yet another magnificent temple. The inside was lit by tiny lights and the god-like effigies were surrounded by awesome gold ornaments.

Back at our accommodation, we were distressed to discover that indeed our privacy had been violated. We came to the conclusion that we had been 'lured' away to enable the room to be searched. This being the case, we reasoned that perhaps it was actually safer for us to be under such scrutiny in this new environment given the amount of interest we were attracting.

Later, the proprietor of the facility invited us to join him at his house and meet his wife and a few of their friends. Once the introductions were over, one of the friends, who happened to be a doctor, suggested we go for a drive with him back to his house, giving us the opportunity to see more of the sights of Bhuj on the way. Interestingly, before we could leave, the doctor had to consult with our police acquaintances, whereupon the decision was made for a police officer to accompany us.

The outing with the doctor could not have been very interesting as it did not appear worthy of noting in the diary. However, when we returned to the hotel for our evening meal, a crowd had gathered at the entrance to watch us. Although we were evidently celebrities, it did not sit comfortably with George or me.

The whole time we were eating our meal in our cubicle-like room, we were aware of the fact there was always a group of men in the adjoining room and we felt sure we were being bugged.

After we'd eaten, I left the room to make a trip to the outside toilet. Much to my horror, I discovered that the young boy who ran the errands for us was sitting with a friend at a vantage point from which they had a clear line of vision into our room. We did not think the police had put them up to it; rather, we thought it probably a youthful curiosity. Regardless, all the scrutiny and intrigue was getting to us and we began to think we were becoming paranoid.

So, to test it out, at 11.00pm George decided to take the guards for a walk, saying he would be gone about twenty minutes. When he hadn't returned over an hour, I started to seriously worry. As such, I dressed and went outside, only to be approached by two police officers asking me if anything was amiss. I told them I was worried and looking for my husband. Just as I finished, two other officers approached and said that George was coming. There was no secret made of the fact that George had been followed. Now we were in no doubt that the men in the adjoining room were watching us; and probably listening as well.

—

Monday 5 August
Bhuj, India

Neither George nor I slept very well at all.

In fact, I was to experience one of the most memorable occurrences of our entire travels. As dawn broke, I stirred out of a dozy sleep and, as I was already facing George's bed, glanced over to see if he was awake. I couldn't believe what I was looking at. As I furiously blinked to clear my vision, I saw quite clearly two figures bending over his bed looking down on him. One had his back to me (I was of the impression he was male) and seemed to be dressed in a white organza, long, loose robe. The other, similarly dressed, was facing me and somehow positioned between the wall and the bed. It should be said both beds were hard up against the walls. I got the impression they were looking down on George and discussing him. I froze for seconds, then very slowly pulled my hand up from under the sheet to grasp the edge of the sheet under my chin. I paused again never taking my eyes off the 'men'. Then as soon as I moved slightly to lower the sheet with the intention of getting up, the figure facing me seemed to glance up and immediately vanished. Almost instantaneously the figure with its back to me also vanished. I was stunned, though oddly enough I wasn't the least bit frightened; rather, I was overwhelmed with a strange sense of relief and elation. By this time George had stirred, so, despite the lack of bed space, I quickly climbed in beside him and stayed there until it was time to rise.

I am not a religious person, and I do not consider myself to be psychic, but I have no rational explanation for that apparition. I only know that after that experience I strongly believed that George had, for want of a better description, 'guardian angels' or some other phenomena looking out for his wellbeing. I also felt quite strongly that we would make it safely to Australia and that there was a yet undisclosed purpose for doing so.

We rose at 9.00am and, after some hesitation, accepted breakfast, which was the first mistake of the day. We were both violently sick as soon as the greasy, oily mess went down.

At the prearranged time, we climbed into the police truck that had come to collect us and were taken to the bank to change traveller's cheques into local money. Still with our full contingency of escorts, we went to the market and purchased a large chamois and a filter to use when we filled Charlie Golf's tanks with petrol.

While at the market, we also splashed out and bought a locally hand-beaten, solid silver trinket box. We reasoned if things went bad for us we could always sell it and recoup the money.

From the market we returned to the airport where we learned that we had permission to travel across India on our original scheduled route as long as we signed an affidavit for the authorities, confirming that Charlie Golf could indeed fly on high octane petrol. Feeling quite buoyant with this new outcome in our favour, our next stop was to get the fuel from the local garage and back to Charlie Golf, using our trusty five-gallon, plastic container.

When we arrived back at our hotel cubicle, we were suddenly invaded by three newspaper reporters from both *Reuters* and the Indian tabloids. Surprisingly, their main interest was confirming the fact that we received permission to continue our travels across India. Earlier in the day George and I had bought a local newspaper that carried photographs of us on the front page, so we took the opportunity to ask the reporters to translate the accompanying story for us. These same reporters also told us of the outlandish rumour that I was an Australian millionairess.

I wish! They also said our story would appear in the *National Press of India* the following day.

Later in the day, we took ourselves out for another sightseeing walk and came across a small St Andrew's Church tucked way down a back street. On closer inspection, it was revealed that this little, well-maintained church was built by a Colonel Law in memory of his wife.

That night before retiring, we stopped over at the proprietor's house and spent a pleasurable half hour chatting with him and his wife. His wife insisted that we have breakfast with them before we were to leave the next morning.

Hand-beaten silver trinket box (9cm x 6cm x 3cm)

Chapter 15

India — From West to East

Torrential rain and a trip to the country

Tuesday 6 August 1968

Bhuj –Ahmedabad, India

Time of departure: 04.54 GMT Flying time: 1hr 56mins

Flying conditions: Fair visibility, turbulent with few showers.

Wind direction and velocity: 300°/20knots.

That morning we rose at 6.00am and joined our hosts for a special farewell breakfast. After some of the worst cuisine we had experienced so far, I was really looking forward to a couple of boiled eggs. I tucked into the first egg with anticipation, but, to my horror, it was almost raw. The egg was lukewarm and the egg-white was still clear and runny. Having been so outspoken about my delight in being served boiled eggs, I had no choice but to smile and eat them, trying desperately to withhold the gagging. George coped a lot better than I did and tried to distract the attention of our hosts away from the expression on my face.

We took our last photographs of Bhuj before our escorts bundled us into the truck and deposited us at the airport.

After a confused and frustrating hour of satisfying the administrative needs of the airport officials, we were finally cleared to take off and head east to Ahmedabad. The take-off was certainly not pretty due to a strong cross wind, but, despite the turbulence and heavy cloud, the short trip to our next destination was relatively incident free.

Charlie Golf's landing on the runway at Ahmedabad could also have been tidier. This time all the officials were waiting for us on the tarmac and, as soon as we rolled to a standstill, we were surrounded. It was a repeat of the last two landings; that is, papers to be completed, passports taken from us with promises that they would be returned and umpteen questions about our intentions. We also had to wait over three hours before we could get Charlie Golf refuelled with avgas.

It was starting to get all too much for George. He finally lost it and blew his top with one particular custom's official over an unopened bottle of whisky. The official demanded that he keep the unopened bottle in his possession while we signed a statement to verify that we had taken all our belongings into town with us. I believe George won that round.

The next argument started when we discovered that the airport officials had ordered a taxi for us just after we landed. Of course, three plus hours later, the taxi was still waiting with its meter running. There was absolutely no way George and I were prepared to pay the exorbitant fare that had accumulated and so another shouting match ensued. The airport authorities refused to pay and tried to wave the taxi driver away telling him that the hotel would cover the cost. Finally, rather than see the hapless taxi driver out of pocket, we relented and coughed up the full fare. Our opinion of the airport officials at that point did not rate very high.

As the arrival of foreigners piloting their own small plane was such a rare occurrence, locals always assumed that we must be rich and, as such, we were again taken to a high priced hotel.

Once settled into the Ritz, we calmed down and relaxed in a very welcome hot bath. After the accommodation of the past few days, this was luxury.

At long last comfortable and refreshed, we ventured onto the streets of Ahmedabad to shop for postcards and other necessities. We were unable to find a shop that sold cards, but we did come across a newspaper stall selling the *Indian Times*. Lo and behold, on the front page of the paper was the heading, *British couple plane freed*. The final sentence stated, *Without waiting any formal communication, Mr Wright flew from Karachi to Bhuj on August 3.*

We added this cutting to the others we had collected in Karachi and Bhuj; one of which described us as, *a young tall slim Briton and his charming wife Kathleen...*

I am not sure that George and I would have described ourselves quite that way.

Back at the Ritz, we enjoyed the best evening meal we'd had for ages, then fell into a very comfortable bed.

—

Wednesday 7 August
Ahmedabad, India

This Wednesday turned out to be just what we needed to regroup. A quiet, relaxing day was spent doing very little. It was most welcome.

The Met report provided by Ahmedabad was unfavourable for visual flight; that is, ground level cloud, thunderstorms and heavy rain-showers. As such, we spent the day catching up on letters to send home to loved ones. As I was feeling somewhat off-colour, I managed to get an afternoon sleep in before we went down to dinner. Neither George nor I ate very much, so we decided to retire early for the night and hopefully better weather would enable us to continue our travels the following morning. With the constant delays, we were becoming more concerned that the monsoons would catch up with us and we would be grounded for months. We did not have the financial resources to cope with that scenario.

—

Thursday 8 August
Ahmedabad, India

We again woke to heavy rain showers, but still went to the airport to check out the projected forecast. Just like the day before, the news was not good, so we returned to the hotel for another day of waiting for the weather to improve. While posting letters we had written the day before and exchanging traveller's cheques, we managed to get a good soaking from the continual heavy downpour.

During the afternoon, a reporter from the *Indian Times* caught up with us and requested an interview with photographs. Then, again in the late afternoon while we were having pre-dinner whiskies, two reporters and a photographer from the *Western Times* asked if we would answer questions for them. As per usual, we obliged. Before they left, the most senior of the three kindly offered to send a car for us the following day to show us the tourist attractions if we were still grounded in Ahmedabad. These interludes with the news media certainly helped to pass the time while we waited for the weather to clear.

That night, in anticipation that we would be on our way to Indore the following morning, we retired early.

—

Friday 9 August
Ahmedabad, India

The thunder, lightning and rain were so spectacular during the night that I dragged George out of bed and onto the veranda to watch. After that we slept in 'til late as it became quite apparent the weather conditions were not conducive for visual flying. This was just as well because George had stomach problems and wasn't feeling the best.

I breakfasted alone, then picked up the daily newspapers to find out what the Indian public was being told about us. The reports were reasonably accurate and we weren't disappointed.

Later in the morning, we telephoned the newspaper editor who had given us his number the previous day. About half an hour later, he arrived at the hotel with two of his friends. We were to learn that one of our new acquaintances was a certain Mr Munshaw, the owner of two textile mills in India and also the director of sports clubs and other associations.

Our first stop was to buy some beer, but, unfortunately, the brand our hosts wanted was not available. The second stop was to Mr Munshaw's magnificent home with a superb, carved-wooden front entrance and beautiful lush gardens. He also had on display some splendid valuable stone carvings, which, we were told, were hundreds of years old. His wife, Nandini, then showed us her solid silver jewellery and gave me some small trinkets to keep.

After this 'show and tell' session, we were taken to Mr Munshaw's club where we wined and dined. We felt very special indeed. Although, having said that, I do recall I embarrassed myself during the main course. I had ordered a mild, curry chicken. I was served with a section of the chicken still on the bone. For me that is the best part, so I picked up a section of chicken with my fingers and started to eat it off the bone. As I pulled it away from my mouth, my finger slipped and a lump of chicken coated in curry sauce flew across the table and splattered our host — bull's eye! I was so embarrassed. There was now a row of yellowy-brown stains all down the front of his dazzling white shirt. I apologised profusely and, if I remember correctly, he had the etiquette to be quite gracious about it.

Having finished our delicious meal, we went to Mr Munshaw's home where his wife made us a cup of tea. Nandini and her friend then took George and me to see a textile museum. As I have always done my own dressmaking, I found the visit extremely enlightening and interesting. We were then shown traditional sari patterns representing the different regions of India. Nandini suggested I might need to dress in a sari when travelling through certain parts of India, so with her help I purchased one and she showed me how to wrap it round my body and how to wear it. As I am 5ft 10in tall, I felt large and cumbersome and clumsy during this process, given the Indian women around me all seemed to be so tiny and petite. The sari I purchased was made of deep pink, fine cotton and embossed with a traditional red border design of elephants.

On the return journey, we were taken to see a famous lattice window carved from stone. Again, quite a spectacular piece of architecture and well worth a few photographs.

In the early evening, our friends collected us from the hotel in a very fancy, turquoise-blue, soft-top sedan and took us to another luxurious villa situated by a river on the outskirts of town. This was the home of Nadini's uncle, sister and mother. We were led to believe that Nandini's uncle was an industrialist and a member of the board of the Bank of India.

We had a superb evening with these very kind people. The dinner was most enjoyable, the drinks kept coming and the conversation was engaging and light-hearted.

During the conversation, we were fascinated to learn that there had been a report printed in Bhuj that claimed we were spies and, as we were collecting articles written about us, we were given a copy of the offending newspaper item that blazed the headline, *SPY PLANE?*

George and I were quite sorry when that evening came to an end as we had so much enjoyed and appreciated the trouble our hosts had taken on our behalf to make our stay in Ahmedabad a pleasant experience.

—

Saturday 10 August
Ahmedabad – Indore, India

Time of departure: 03.32 GMT Flying time: 2hrs 09mins
Flying conditions: Heavy rain, low cloud, poor visibility. Wind direction and velocity: 270°/25knots.

We were quite reluctant to get out of bed this morning, but, after a coffee, we were soon on our way to the airport once more. The Met report was more favourable for our type of flying, so we decided we would push on to Indore. We had everything ready and in order when the custom's officer decided there was a problem that had to be resolved before we could leave Ahmedabad and, as usual, the problem involved parting with yet more money. Apparently, the officials in Bhuj had neglected to charge us some sort of duty over and above the amount that was debited to our fuel carnet. Before embarking on our journey, we had purchased a carnet (similar to the modern credit card, but quite a unique system in 1968) from a well-known, international fuel company before we left Scotland. As we travelled through the different countries, the carnet enabled us to purchase fuel without having to use cash. Anyway, the custom's officials would not let us leave until we had paid our debt.

This 'hold up', metaphorically speaking, delayed our flight for over an hour.

Because of the improved weather conditions, the airport was

busy with extra flights and the comings and goings of emergency relief helicopters servicing the flooded areas with food parcels; another stark reminder of the monsoon conditions chasing us. This extra airport activity and our delayed take-off time added to the difficulties of visual flight conditions.

The flight to Indore was not comfortable and at times we were dropping to around 500ft to sneak under heavy rain clouds. Approximately ten minutes out from Indore, a gap opened up in the cloud enabling us to locate the airport and join downwind for a perfect landing.

On landing, we were informed that we would have to wait over two hours for fuel and that India Oil would only accept cash as the company didn't recognise our fuel carnet. This meant we would have to change traveller's cheques as George didn't think we had enough ready rupees.

As often happened in our travels, the airport superintendent took us under his wing and ran us into the city in his Jeep to find a bank. On the way back to the airport, we had lunch and beers in a rather classy, eighty rupees a night hotel. Our new friend treated us to lunch and we bought the beers. We then stopped off at the superintendent's lodgings at the Lanteen Hotel. He was paying eight rupees a night for a fairly reasonable room. Given that the refuelling of Charlie Golf would not be possible for at least three more hours, we whiled away the time in the Lanteen Hotel. George decided that it was quite adequate accommodation for us, so we booked in for the night.

After all the necessary tasks had been seen to with Charlie Golf and the airport officials, we took ourselves off to bed. Unfortunately, our room was located right over the hotel kitchen, but with the constant clattering noise penetrating the floor and flimsy walls, sleep was a long time coming.

—

Sunday 11 August
Indore — Nagpur, India
Time of departure: 03.31 GMT   Flying time: 3hrs
Flying conditions: Heavy rain, low cloud, poor visibility. Wind direction and velocity: 270°/25knots.

We were delighted to see an improvement in the weather that morning and looked forward to three hours of fair weather flying. We took a taxi back to the airport. At 9.00am, while we were still waiting patiently to pay the fuel company representative for the fuel we had purchased the previous day, the president of the Indore Royal Flying Club kindly invited us to join a group of members for coffee. It was a welcome distraction. We were presented with small, metal, club badges and memorabilia of the 1965 Indian Aero Club Conference.

In order to hasten our departure, we left a message with the flying club to the effect that we would pay for the fuel we had received when we arrived in Nagpur. Unfortunately, the air traffic controllers would not grant us clearance to take off until they had double-checked the payment arrangement, with the result we were sitting out on the airport apron with Charlie Golf's engine idling for well over fifteen minutes.

Eventually, we were given permission to take off and, on the advice of the local pilots of the flying club, decided to follow the high tension power lines to Nagpur. What they failed to tell me was that the pylons stopped short of Nagpur at a reservoir in the mountains. Having moved away from our original flight path, I had trouble picking up the tracking features on the ground, with the result I could not accurately pin-point our exact location. The weather was beginning to close in and so it was a relief when Nagpur picked us up on the radio transmitter as quickly as they did. When we received the directions to the airport, it turned out that we had been following the correct heading and were spot-on course.

The fuel problem was perpetuated at Nagpur. The oil company representative was initially happy to accept and process our fuel carnet, that is, until he received a telephone call from Indore that immediately changed his mind. We paid this rep for the fuel we received there as well as the fuel we had purchased in Indore. Debt paid.

Over sandwiches and coffee in the restaurant, we decided we would part with the Rp8 and spend the night in the airport rest-room accommodation. These quarters were very comfortable and well maintained for the price. I also managed to buy post-cards and get them on their way despite the fact it was Sunday.

It was a balmy cool afternoon, so we went for a walk through the streets of Nagpur then lazily watched the Indian Air Force gliders soaring in the skies above us. We knew exactly what it felt like to be up there.

We had a very light evening meal before returning to our room for the night.

—

Monday 12 August
Nagpur, India

I woke early feeling quite ill and squeamish. We were taking regular doses of anti-malaria tablets and I was beginning to think they were having an adverse reaction on my guts.

At 5.00am local time, I woke George and we got ready to leave the accommodation even though I was unsure as to whether or not I was fit to travel. As we were packing, George noticed a large, ugly-looking scorpion lurking behind the bath-room door. We kept well away from it.

The weather forecast provided by the Met office at the

Nagpur Airport indicated a deep depression over Ranchi/Calcutta that was rapidly travelling west. Although we could probably safely make the two-hour trip to Raipur before the bad weather set in, once it did, we could expect to be grounded in Raipur for several days. This being the case, we decided that it would be more sensible to wait out the bad weather here in Nagpur where we were guaranteed cheap, comfortable accommodation.

The decision made, we returned to the rest house. I had packed the left-over, used soap, thinking that it would not be left for the next guests to use. Wrong! When we returned to our room, the cleaner held out her hand and asked for the used soap back. I felt like a thief caught in the act. It hadn't occurred to me that I was probably depriving the cleaner of one of her perks.

Once settled back in the room, I took myself off to bed as I was still feeling quite ill.

It was a change to be in a part of the world where private flying clubs were common, so George left me to sleep and took the opportunity to catch up with fellow pilots. He befriended a young Sikh who took him for a spin in his own single-engine aircraft.

After a sandwich lunch, we were again invaded by reporters, photographers and the Sikh who George had befriended earlier. In the several photographs taken during that afternoon, I appeared quite melancholy, much thinner and with my hair considerably longer than when we first left Scotland. George also appeared to have lost a lot of weight. In newspaper articles I had been described as "charming wife", "charming, golden-haired bride" and "vivacious". That Monday a better description would have been "death warmed up".

Regardless, we politely answered all the questions put to us and posed for the photographs beside Charlie Golf. George also accepted his friend's invitation for us to have dinner that night. I didn't feel quite up to it, but, as George was eager to go, we made ourselves presentable by the time the car collected us at 6.30pm.

As it turned out, the evening was a success. George and his three male companions consumed a full bottle of whisky while the womenfolk dressed me up in a sari. The diary notes indicate that we had a hilarious evening. This is despite the fact that I had a very difficult time refusing food. Our Sikh hosts would not take no for an answer.

Feeling unwell and exhausted, I was relieved to get back into bed that night as I had quite enough of socialising for a while.

During the evening, one of the newspaper reporters offered to take us the next day to meet some Scottish medics who were working in the missions and the local hospital.

—

Tuesday 13 August
Nagpur, India

We experienced yet another night of poor sleep. We were also reminded that according to our planned schedule, we should have been in Australia by this time.

Our newspaper friend arrived at precisely 8.00am with Reverend Reg Coates, a minister of the Scottish church who ran an orphanage and a school for Indian children. Reverend Coates was small in stature but a lively character with plenty of energy. We learned that he arrived in India with absolutely nothing and had over the years built the mission from the ground up. We also learned that the newspaper reporter who had befriended us was a recent convert from Hindu to Christianity. Both George and I were non-practising Protestants, so religious matters were of no great consequence to us. However, we were quite respectful of others' beliefs.

Our first stop in the Jeep was for breakfast in the centre of Nagpur. Next stop was to Reverend Coates' home where we were introduced to his wife. Our mode of transport changed to a taxi and on our way to the Yerdla Orphanage School we were joined by another of the Reverend's friends. Reverend Moss was also a doctor who ran a mission some 300kms out of Nagpur.

As we were shown round the orphanage, the children at Yerdla were curious to see us and showed great interest in our travels. On leaving, we were presented with an Indian doll that the children had made. The doll was approximately 10in high, dressed in orange traditional costume for that region and carrying a basket of seeds on her head. It was a touching thought and a great memento.

It was as we were leaving Yerdla that Reverend Moss asked if we cared to spend a few days with him at the mission up in the Indian jungle. We knew we were grounded for at least two days, so rather than while away the time in the rest house, we gratefully accepted his invitation.

Our next stop was at the Muir Memorial Hospital where we were introduced to Scottish doctors and nurses who showed us around wards. It all seemed rather strange to us to see the relatives of patients camped on rugs beside the beds with all their cooking gear and bedding. This was hospitalisation, Indian style.

Once back in our sleeping quarters, I quickly packed all our gear while George made arrangements with the airport staff to have Charlie Golf securely housed during our absence.

With heads still full of our morning encounters, we were bundled back into the Jeep by our newspaper guides and taken to a restaurant where we met up again with the Reverends Coates and Moss.

The rain was still coming down in sheets when we bade farewell to Reverend Coates and our acquaintances. Reverend Moss had more errands to run before we left Nagpur. The last call was to another hospital to collect a patient suffering from TB (tuberculosis). This hospital was operated by the Catholic Church and specialised in paralysis. Once again we were shown through the wards and introduced to the staff. Being quite unfamiliar with such environments, George and I were amazed at the apparatus used to help and support the paralysed patients.

After what seemed a long day, we eventually left Nagpur by car and embarked on the three-hour journey through the awe-inspiring, lush, green countryside and up to the mission at Padhar. Despite the continuous rain, we sighted several monkeys en-route. Arriving at Padhar tired and travel-weary, we were still able to appreciate the beauty and isolation of the bungalows set in the midst of dense jungle.

We settled in quickly, refreshed ourselves in our new surroundings then went to dinner. We spent the rest of the evening drinking coffee and learning about the local exotic animals from Reverend Moss. We were told the surrounding forests were home to brown bears, tigers, panthers and deer, to name but a few.

We were exhausted but relaxed and happy when we retired for the night. In this environment we could forget about flying to Australia for just a little while.

Wednesday 14 August
Nagpur, India

The heavy rain pounding on the tin roof kept me awake most of the night and at 7.30am we were brought to life by Reverend Moss playing familiar rousing hymns on the organ. It was quite a unique but pleasant experience for George and I.

During that morning, with the rain still teeming and dressed in my sari, I caught up with correspondence, washing and other necessary chores. The rest of the afternoon we enjoyed the luxury of being able to laze on the veranda and read.

At around 4.00pm, we were taken to the Olivers' house for afternoon tea. The Olivers was an Irish couple who worked for Reverend Moss on the mission. We all came together for the evening meal. A minister from Sweden had also joined the company and so the rest of the evening was spent quietly discussing politics and religion.

Before turning in for the night, I checked on our washing, only to discover that although it was hanging up under cover, it was still as wet as it was when I hung it up earlier that morning.

—

Thursday 15 August
Nagpur, India

Severe indigestion, heartburn and stomach pains kept me awake most of the night. I finally dozed off, but in the morning I was still feeling ill. Reluctant to make a fuss, I mentioned my malady to Reverend Moss and he gave me a couple of tablets to ease my suffering. By this time I was convinced the anti-malaria tablets were the cause and decided to stop taking them.

It was still raining heavily, so there wasn't a great deal George and I could do except relax and read on the veranda. After lunch, Reverend Moss told us he would take us to see the considerably large power station situated approximately fifty miles north of Padhar as he had some pickups to do in that area.

The drive north was scenic and enjoyable. At a river ford we came upon an Esso oil tanker stuck in the mud up to its back axle. A truck that appeared to have been trying to rescue the oil tanker was also bogged up to its back axle in sand. Reverend Moss stopped to see if we could be of assistance and made a couple of attempts at pulling the truck out of the sand with the Jeep but to no avail. He then decided we would tackle the ford crossing and, much to our delight, we reached the other side with very little effort.

We continued over the rough, pot-holed roads until we reached the power station located against a backdrop of impressive, lush, green, mountainous scenery. We were shown round the station workings and then Reverend Moss delivered a letter to the station manager at his home. We were fed with tea and biscuits and made to feel very welcome.

Reverend Moss' next job was to call in on an American couple, Mr and Mrs Stoll, to collect a cooker to take back with us to Padhar. On the way, we stopped to gaze in awe at the huge dam and the beautiful lake behind it.

After a bit of to-ing and fro-ing, Reverend Moss located the Stolls enjoying a celebratory gathering for Indian Independence. By this time it was getting dark, so George, Reverend Moss and Mr Stoll wasted no time in loading the cooker onto the back of the Jeep. The rain was coming down in sheets when we eventually left the mountains to return to Padhar and we started to feel anxious about the Jeep's ability to cross the ford on the way back. We picked up another local traveller on the road who had become stranded because of the rain.

When we reached the ford, we were relieved to discover that the river level had not yet been affected by the rain. Notwithstanding, there were another two trucks blocking the road on our side of the ford. After getting out and giving the situation a cursory inspection, Reverend Moss decided to risk driving off the road to circumvent the trucks and then take the Jeep across the ford. The petrol tanker we had seen before was still stuck fast in the sandy mud, but now there were half a dozen men trying to lever the back axle free with a long, sturdy pole.

Reverend Moss expertly nursed the Jeep through the ford and, with the rest of the journey somewhat uneventful, we arrived at Padhar tired and hungry but in a very jovial mood.

After the evening meal, Reverend Moss contacted the Met office in Nagpur and requested a long term weather forecast. Much to our delight, we learned that the bad weather was abating to the point where we should be able to resume our travels on Saturday. This being the case, we would have had to leave for Nagpur the following day.

Perhaps I hadn't fully recovered from my ailments, but that night I was afflicted with a serious, depressing bout of homesickness. It seemed so long since we'd been in touch with loved ones and I was missing them. I cried myself to sleep.

—

Friday 16 August
Nagpur, India

Our mode of transport today was to be by train from Betul to Nagpur.

We both had a good night's sleep so we awoke refreshed and ready for another day's travels. Reverend Moss had already been to the hospital to perform early morning surgery by the time George and I had packed the cases and breakfasted.

The Olivers invited us to have lunch with them before we were taken to the station by Jeep. It was to be another sad and tearful goodbye as we had become very friendly with all our host families. We also greatly appreciated their hospitality.

The train was almost two hours late arriving in Betul, but it wasn't a problem. George and I climbed aboard and settled ourselves into a second class compartment. The train was as we had anticipated — wooden slat seats, bars over the supposed windows with no glass and no partition separating seats from the corridor. Nevertheless, it was adequate for our purposes and we whiled away the four hours reading and enjoying the passing scenery.

Once back in Nagpur, we took a taxi straight to the airport guest house and this ended in the usual raging argument with the driver over the cost of the fare. Eventually we managed to negotiate a fare acceptable to both parties.

As we were tucking into an evening meal of chicken, omelette and coffee, the representative from India Oil approached and, much to our delight, advised us that we had been overcharged for our fuel and that we were due a rebate. We needn't have been so excited as the rebate turned out to be all of one rupee and fifty cents (about one shilling and sixpence). After our meal, we posted cards and then wandered over to the hangar to ensure all was in order with Charlie Golf and to get a formal Met report for the morning.

We had planned on going straight to bed. However, just as I was dropping off to sleep George's pilot acquaintance from the flying club turned up. I stayed in bed and managed to drop off to sleep, only to wake an hour later with severe stomach pains again. I lay awake for ages listening to George and his friend talking and drinking in the next room.

After the guest left, George was not in the best frame of mind. One harsh word led to another and he accused me of faking the illness to seek sympathy. I was devastated and could only think it was the drink talking. The result was I took my pillow and blanket and tried to make myself comfortable in the other room while I made numerous trips back and forth to the toilet. The hands of the clock seemed to take forever to reach 5.00am, the time at which the alarm was set.

—

Saturday 17 August
Nagpur — Raipur, India
Time of departure: 01.31 GMT Flying time: 2hrs 05mins
Flying conditions: Heavy rain, low cloud, poor visibility. Wind direction and velocity: 220°/25knots.

After the fiasco of the previous evening, I had no choice but to go along with the day's travel plans. Anyway, I was getting no relief lying in bed.

We managed to carry out all the airport administrative requirements within a reasonable space of time before taking Charlie Golf to the skies after almost six days of languishing on the tarmac.

Because of the low cloud and threatening weather, we decided we would follow the railway line at an altitude of 500–1000ft. After only two hours, we located the airfield and executed a perfect landing. Once on the ground, we made several telephone calls and waited for four hours before the captain of the Raipur Flying Club arrived with the fuel. By the time we had taxied to the club hanger and refuelled Charlie Golf, it was clearly too late to continue. This was becoming the norm in India.

When the flying club closed for the afternoon, the captain gave us a lift in his Jeep to the Gass Memorial Centre in town where we booked in for the night. The price was most reasonable and the room comfortable.

I was feeling a great deal better by this time and so we ordered omelette and coffee for tea. We were brought coffees, but no omelettes. Rather than make a fuss, we wandered down the street to another eating place and bought some sandwiches.

Later in the evening, the captain of the Aero Club called in to tell us he had arranged to have us collected and taken to the airfield at 6.00am the following morning.

—

Sunday 18 August

Raipur — Jamshedpur, India

Time of departure: 04.47 GMT Flying time: 3hrs 19mins
Flying conditions: Warm, low cloud, thunderstorms. Wind direction and velocity: 240°/20knots.

Feeling refreshed from a great night's sleep and no more stomach pains, I felt on top of the world that morning and was quite looking forward to getting on our way again. George too was in good spirits. By the appointed time of 6.00am, we had eaten, packed and were waiting for our promised lift to the airport. At 8.00am we were still waiting and all the positive feelings had vanished. Our tempers rising, George decided to hail the nearest three-wheel rickshaw and get ourselves to the airport. With two adults and all our baggage, it was not only a squeeze, but a very bumpy and uncomfortable ride. However, it served the purpose and got us to the airport.

Once at the airport, we experienced yet more delays as it took forever to get a Met report, pay fees and finalise the flight plan. At 10.00am local time, we were taxiing Charlie Golf to the runway ready for take-off. More problems! Charlie Golf developed a magneto drop that took well over five minutes to clear. After a very frustrating start to the day, we eventually took off at 10.19am local time.

The rainstorms were much more severe than predicted in the Met report received at Raipur, but we managed to duck under the worst of them. Jamshedpur airport came into sight right on schedule. However, when we joined downwind, the air traffic controller informed us that the runway was under repair and we would have to land on the threshold. George slightly misjudged our altitude on the first approach, so he pulled the joy stick back and executed an overshoot. His second attempt to land Charlie Golf was successful.

Jamshedpur from the tarmac looked promising. The airport seemed much bigger and with more amenities than we'd been afforded in the last few days of flying, including Burma Shell fuelling facilities.

Our initial plan when we set out in the morning was to try for two trips and get to Calcutta that same day. Again, by the time we had refuelled Charlie Golf and completed the other airport paperwork, it was getting too late in the day to risk a second flight. Instead, we tied our aircraft down for the night and took a taxi into the main town.

This time we booked into a classier hotel where we could enjoy the luxury of hot showers. After freshening up, it was down to the bar for sandwiches and beer. While we were enjoying our snack, a member of the Jamshedpur Aero Club telephoned and arranged to meet us at the hotel at 6.00pm. George and I stayed in the bar relaxing, drinking and feeling quite amorous. However, when the supposed company hadn't arrived by 7.30, we got tired of waiting and so wandered into the hotel restaurant for our evening meal. Lo and behold, the gentlemen who we were waiting for were already in the dining room tucking into their dinners. We were ushered to their table feeling somewhat disgruntled and invited to join them. Neither George nor I felt like we wanted to. However, rather than appear rude, we accepted.

We were to learn that the two joint owners of the hotel at which we were staying were among the company. After chatting for a while, our acquaintances took us to a rather exclusive nightclub for more drinking and socialising. We then all returned to our hotel. By this time George and I had had far too much alcohol and so we decided it was time to eat something substantial.

The five or six of us sat down to order and then suddenly all but one disappeared and didn't return; and so, without any explanations, George and I were left in the company of just one aero club member. Having eaten and ridding ourselves of our so-called companion, we took ourselves up to bed.

—

Monday 19 August
Jamshedpur, India

This time the discomfort and middle-of-the-night thirst was most definitely self-inflicted. We had hoped to be up and on our way early, but we had to wait for the banks to open so we could change traveller's cheques and pay the hotel bill.

Over breakfast, we made the decision to stay in Jamshedpur for the day as neither of us really felt fit enough for flying and the weather was getting hot again. Calcutta would have to wait until tomorrow.

On arrival at the hotel the day before, we got the impression that the receptionist treated us with disdain and so when we were called back to the reception desk that morning and asked if we would like to move to a more comfortable room that had air conditioning, we were quite amused. We could only guess that the receptionist, seeing us in the company of the owners the previous evening, thought it best to upgrade our accommodation arrangements.

We settled into our new surroundings, then did some forward flight planning. After studying the maps, we were pleased to discover that we could easily get from Calcutta to Chittagong without having to land and refuel at Dacca.

Now flush with money, we went to the airport to file our flight plan to Calcutta and send a signal to East Pakistan requesting permission to enter their air space and land at Chittagong.

While doing a routine check on Charlie Golf, George discovered that the magneto was still giving trouble and so on the first hot sunny day we'd experienced for ages, George was out on the tarmac doing running repairs on the aircraft. He discovered that one of the plugs was oiled up. However; using the airport engineers' equipment, he was able to clean it. It was obviously the attention the Gypsy Major engine needed, because when George was finished, it started up and ran like a dream.

Hot and exhausted, we returned to the hotel and caught up with the other necessary chores.

Dinner that evening was spent in a very romantic frame of mind, with the two of us reminiscing earlier times and laughing over past crazy situations we had got ourselves into and somehow managed to get out of. Our love and respect for each other was rekindled.

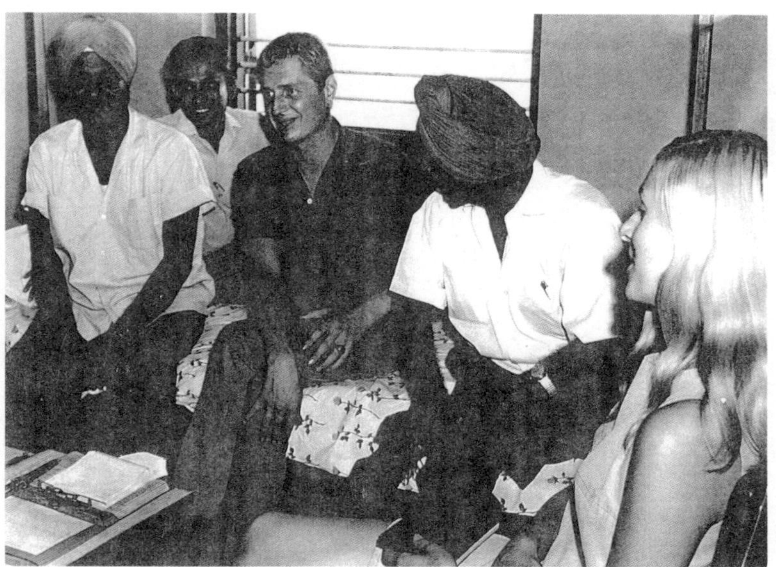

Inquisitive friends (log book and flight-plan paperwork at bottom left)

Kate and George answering questions during an interview session

Chapter 16

India — Calcutta

Arrested for spying and in trouble with the authorities

Tuesday 20 August 1968
Jamshedpur — Calcutta, India
Time of departure: 01.34 GMT Flying time: 2hrs 32mins
Flying conditions: Hot, low cloud, mist. Wind direction and velocity: 160°/10knots.

We woke at 5.00am local time, had coffee, paid the hotel bill and took a taxi to Jamshedpur airport. Despite the overnight thunderstorms, that day's flying conditions were looking good. For a pleasant change, it didn't take long to clear the airport administration and we were soon on our way to Calcutta. We were both in an excellent frame of mind and the navigation was straight-forward. I should have known better.

At an estimated twenty miles out of Calcutta, George attempted to raise Dum Dum International Airport on the radio transmitter. We could hear the air traffic controllers very clearly as they directed the International 'big boys' through their landing and take-off procedures. However, it soon became apparent that Dum Dum controllers were not receiving our signals. Not a good situation to be in when approaching an international airport with a very heavy traffic load. George tried circling and taking Charlie Golf up to 5,000ft to see if height would give us better transmission, but to no avail.

Then, following the internationally accepted procedure to alert the air traffic controllers and their radar system of our presence, George proceeded to fly Charlie Golf in a triangle formation on the perimeter of the airport. To our dismay, this manoeuvre went unnoticed and we got no response.

By this time we were getting very concerned about our situation, as we could still receive Dum Dum transmissions quite clearly. For safety reasons, our only option was to divert to the nearest alternative airfield. Frantically checking the topographical map, I located an airstrip a few miles north-west of Dum Dum.

On closer inspection, we agreed that this alternative would be our best option while still trying desperately to get our radio transmitter to function correctly. By this time, we were baffled as we had not experienced any major communication breakdowns before.

With both of us keeping vigilant visual flight, George brought Charlie Golf down to 1,500ft and we followed the river on a north-westerly course to the identified airfield. It was while George was circling and checking out the local traffic that we realised that the airstrip we had chosen was in fact a military one. This came as quite a surprise as that level of detail was not shown on the topographical map I was using.

As George took Charlie Golf downwind and waggled the wings, as was the accepted procedure for undeclared arrivals, we both quite clearly sighted a green flag being waved from the control tower, the recognised signal giving us permission to land. George turned onto final approach and brought Charlie Golf down to land. However, with the strong cross wind and his concentration interrupted with looking for signals and other aircraft, the first attempt was too fast and hard, so George aborted the landing, opened the throttle and went round again. The green flag was still displayed. Just as the wheels touched the tarmac a second time we saw a figure on the control tower pull down the green flag and replace it with a red one which meant we did not have permission to land. George pulled back the joystick and lifted off again without stopping.

It was then we heard over our radio transmitter the air traffic controller at Dum Dum calling for the aircraft located north of the international airport to identify itself. We were overcome with relief as we realised that Dum Dum now had us on radar. We were directed to identify ourselves with several simple manoeuvres and then given compass headings to follow that took us straight on to the dead side of the International Civil Airport. Once over the airport, the radio transmission rectified itself and we could communicate clearly with air traffic control. Feeling quite relieved, George joined downwind and, considering the circumstances, made an excellent landing.

However, this relief was to be short lived, as our troubles had just begun.

We were to learn that a Pan Am passenger jet had inadvertently landed at the military airfield only a few weeks before and as the airfield was supposedly top secret it caused a diplomatic furore.

As soon as Charlie Golf rolled to a halt in the allotted parking bay, we were physically removed from the aircraft by officers who we believed were from the Indian Air Force, separated, and then officiously escorted to different rooms where we were coolly but politely interrogated for up to four hours without a break.

The officers took possession of all our undeveloped rolls of negatives and all the movie films we had taken in the past two months telling us that, if nothing untoward was found on them, they would be returned to us in Australia. We were absolutely devastated. Although there was nothing at all suspicious about our photographs, we knew we probably would not see them again and the loss of all those precious photos and 8mm film footage was almost unbearable. When writing my diary I had not described scenery and people in detail as I was relying on the pictures themselves to prompt the memories.

Also, unbeknown to us at the time, while the interrogators held us against our will and away from our aircraft, other officers inspected, searched and ransacked Charlie Golf, looking for spy cameras, hidden devices, or any other evidence that might prove we were into the business of spying.

By mid-afternoon, we were brought together once more and asked the same questions over and over again. Anxious, tired, and hungry and before the Indian customs officers took over, we were eventually allowed to go to the airport dining area to eat. Somehow we managed to take deep breaths and relax our guard a little. After all, we had nothing to hide.

We went through the same interrogation procedures with both the police and customs, although they weren't nearly as forceful and demanding as the military officers had been. We did learn from customs officers that we would receive a rebate on all the fuel we had purchased in India, but I think that was the only positive information we received since we landed in Dum Dum that morning.

While George was still completing custom's forms I walked across the airport apron and booked into the airport guest house. I was assured that our accommodation had air-conditioning, but when I was shown the room, there was no air conditioning and there were windows with no glass in them. I returned to reception and kicked up a storm. I was so angry.

I was then given a room that was a great deal better, although still not air-conditioned.

I just got settled when George arrived. By now it was after 6.00pm and we still hadn't completed the report for air traffic control, nor had we refuelled Charlie Golf. We had learned, however, that the authorities in East Pakistan had responded to our earlier signal seeking permission to enter their country by asking questions to which we had already supplied the answers.

George left me to have a shower while he went to finalise the paperwork and fuel the aircraft. Feeling apprehensive when he hadn't returned for over two hours, I walked over to the apron. Apparently the authorities had initially refused to allow him to refuel Charlie Golf and it was only after a very heated shouting match that they relented and the fuel was provided.

Once back in our room, we prepared a signed statement of the day's fiasco and presented it to the officers in the flight briefing room.

By this time, we were utterly and completely mentally and physically exhausted and very, very hot, so sleep did not come easy that night.

—

Wednesday 21 August
Calcutta, India

George woke me at 6.00am to tell me he was going across to Charlie Golf to try and fix the radio. I slept 'til 9.00 and then went to join George. I hunted all over the airport, but couldn't find him, so I returned to the guest house.

At air traffic control I had picked up a signal granting us permission to enter East Pakistan, so once back in our room I collated the information and prepared for our next flight. I was interrupted by a knock on the door. I opened the door to find the guest house bearer with two policemen. The police officers wanted to know where George had gone. I suddenly realised that while searching for George I had been followed. Becoming somewhat irritated, I told them if they wanted to know where George was then they would have to look for him themselves. After they left I thought I'd do another reconnoitre on my own. I, along with a shadow, happened to find George at the airport's main entrance. George was quite annoyed to learn we were being followed, so we decided to go to the security police office. Once there, we demanded to speak to the superior in charge. George spoke with him on the telephone and was told that there had been a misunderstanding and the shadows would be removed immediately.

Feeling relieved, we breakfasted, then returned to talk to the ground engineers. We learned that the radio had a malfunctioning valve in the transmitter and that a bearer had been sent to Calcutta to get a replacement. We were to be advised later that day if a new valve had been located.

Back in our rooms trying to relax, we were again disturbed by two police officers wanting to ask questions. George told them we had answered all the questions for them the day before and we did not want to go through that interrogation again. The officers eventually left, although they were not at all pleased. George and I then decided we needed new books to read and so wandered over to the terminal building newsagency. We were stopped by the same two police officers who asked us to speak to Mr Campbell their superior officer. Mr Campbell listened intently to our story and subsequent complaints and when we were finished we were told that we would have no more trouble.

We were only back in our room for about an hour when two different officers came knocking and wanting to ask questions. This time George refused point blank to speak to them and sent them packing with a few choice descriptives. He then went back to see Mr Campbell, only to find all of the six officers sitting with him round the desk. Was this some sort of conspiracy?

George was livid and a shouting match commenced with insults thrown back and forth. With nothing gained, we left; and it was no surprise to realise we were once again being followed.

In the afternoon, we decided to go into Calcutta ourselves and headed across to the taxi rank. Every time we tried to hail a taxi, the police officer intervened and told the taxi driver not to take us. We were fuming.

In absolute rage, we went to find an officer of the Indian Air Force to see if they could assist us. We were told that the Air Force had no jurisdiction or influence over police matters and that perhaps it would be best if we contacted the British High Commission for advice.

By this time the weather had broken and the rain was coming down in torrents.

We duly telephoned the British High Commission and were told that if no return contact was made within five minutes we were to ring another number. Fifteen minutes and a couple of beers later, George rang the second number. The person on the other end of the telephone wasn't much help and didn't seem to think he could get us away from the airport. He suggested we ring again in the morning. George was so angry he slammed the telephone down.

By this time, I was getting annoyed and upset with George as it seemed to me he had lost the ability to think rationally. This being the case, I telephoned the High Commission back and spoke with the person myself. I politely and somewhat apologetically explained our plight. He instructed me to contact the senior personnel of the Bengal Police in Calcutta. I had to make another attempt at getting a taxi and if we were refused I was to return to the airport police and ask the reason why we were being forbidden to go into the city.

When I relayed the instructions to George, he flatly refused to go back out in the torrential rain to speak to the police again. By this time I was losing my temper with George and, of course, we ended up having a raging argument. Insults and unkind accusations were thrown on both sides. George even threatened to send me on to Australia by commercial airlines and went so far as to enquire the cost of a flight from the Qantas booking desk.

We ended the day angry, depressed, tired and refusing to communicate with each other.

I even thought that to walk away from this so-called "romantic adventure" here in Calcutta and fly to my brother in Adelaide in the comfort of commercial airlines might not be such a bad idea after all.

—

Thursday 22 August
Calcutta, India

Neither of us slept well and that morning we were very cool with each other. When we went to breakfast, we were still being followed, so George went one way and I the other. In the depressed mood we were in, the distraction provided a little amusement and broke the ice between us.

Later in the morning, we learned that we were still under scrutiny by the Indian Air Force, therefore clearance to resume our flight was pending. Also the ground engineer informed us that they had been unable to procure a replacement radio valve in the city. George decided the only course of action we had was to send a telegram to Mr Simmins, our spare parts contact in the Beagle Terrier company in Britain asking him as a matter of urgency to send a radio valve to us in Calcutta. Our next task was to feed a gallon of engine oil into the Gypsy Major engine.

These tasks completed, we tried our luck at getting a taxi to the British High Commission in the city. Back at the taxi rank, the fiasco of the previous day was repeated with the police officer refusing to allow a driver to accept our fare. Fortunately, an English speaking gentleman saw what was happening and intervened on our behalf, acting as an interpreter. By this time, a crowd had gathered to see what the shouting was about and it appeared to us as if the mob was taking our side. It was most likely probably because the situation was escalating and becoming unmanageable that the police officer relented and allowed us to leave the airport by taxi.

We were very grateful for the English gentleman's intervention and the support of the onlookers.

When we arrived at the office of the British High Commission, we got the distinct feeling we had been expected. It became obvious that, as a result of our contact telephone calls the previous day, the Commission had conducted its own enquiries regarding our situation and the police had denied all knowledge of the incidents relating to the taxis. However, we were given the name of yet another senior police officer to call on. This officer passed us on to a third more senior officer.

We had difficulty locating the latter officer's headquarters, but, when we did, we realised we were now probably in the company of the big bosses. While waiting, we overheard some telephone conversations. From the little we could understand, it was apparent that someone had stepped out of line. Whether it was us or the airport police we were unable to determine.

After waiting forty-five minutes, we were ushered into the office of Superintendent of Police for the Bengal State. He listened politely as we related our experiences and then asked us what seemed to be a number of irrelevant pointless questions. Midway through our meeting, he interrupted George's protestations, rang a bell and calmly ordered tea and coffee to be brought. It was obvious he was not interested in any complaints we put to him. Finally, he promised to investigate the matter thoroughly and assured us we would have no more problems from the police. We thanked the superintendent for taking the trouble to look into our concerns and took our leave.

Now that we were away from the airport, we thought we deserved the luxury of a bit of shopping and sightseeing, so we headed off to Newmarket. Newmarket and the shops did not meet our expectations, but I did get to look at some very beautiful saris. I was shown a magnificent black sari interwoven with gold threads, but the price was quite exorbitant and well out of our purchasing price. I felt a little disappointed, but that was short-lived.

As it was getting quite late, we took a taxi back to the airport and dined in the airport restaurant before retiring for the night.

—

Friday 23 August
Calcutta, India

The following morning, after a very unsettled night, I worked out my frustrations by washing a pile of our dirty clothes and writing up in the diary the events of the past two days. The rest of the morning we spent reading in our room. I was reading one of my favourite books, *A Tale of Two Cities* by Charles Dickens. I bought it because I knew it would keep me engrossed when I needed to forget about the situation I currently found myself in.

In the afternoon, we checked with the Customs Department regarding the importation of the radio valve. It was here we first met Guy Phillips, an Anglo-Indian customs officer who was to become a very dear friend. Guy was able to take us to the correct personnel for the information we needed. We learned that there shouldn't be any restrictions importing the valve as it was our intention to take it out of the country again with us.

Later in the afternoon, while we were sitting outside the room reading, we were visited by the airport manager. He advised us that he had received news from the Director General of Civil Aviation in Delhi that we were cleared to leave Calcutta Dum Dum airport at our earliest convenience. On hearing this great news, we thought it prudent to send back a signal explaining that our departure would be temporarily delayed pending the arrival of a replacement radio valve from Britain.

Later we wandered back over to the airport terminal and met up with Guy Phillips for a coffee.

We were in much better spirits when we retired that evening.

—

Saturday 24 August
Calcutta, India

George awoke to find himself covered in mosquito bites, the result of not sleeping under the net for the past two nights. However, we did notice that the weather was decidedly cooler than it had been since we arrived in Calcutta.

This was to be another morning of lazing around, reading and completing mundane chores, with only two interruptions.

The first was a visit from Mr Campbell, the senior security police officer. Mr Campbell invited us to accompany him to Banackpoc to retrieve our cameras. We refused the offer as the Indian Air Force, although confiscating and destroying our films, had already returned our cameras.

The second was the guest house bearer seeking payment of our accommodation bill.

After lunching in the terminal restaurant, we wandered over to the British Overseas Airways Corporation (BOAC) office to see if the radio valve had arrived on the latest flight. It had not.

We then decided to check on Charlie Golf and, much to our surprise, we discovered the armed guard had been removed. On inspection, we were shocked and appalled to see that the aircraft had been completely ransacked. Paper money had been stolen from George's flying suit. Some of the safety devices from our life jackets were missing and the seals in others were broken. The jackets themselves were badly damaged. We also found that the zips over several of the aircraft frame inspection points had not closed correctly.

While we were assessing the level of theft and damage, Mr Campbell drove up in his Jeep to give George a receipt for the confiscated films. When told of the break-in, he simply shrugged and told us to give him a written report.

When we approached the air traffic controllers, we were told that it was nothing to do with them as the aircraft had been the responsibility of the Police and the Indian Air Force. The Customs Department flatly refused to give us a statement confirming that Charlie Golf had been searched and, for our trouble, we received a lot of abuse from the custom's officer in charge.

Officers of the Indian Air Force said it had nothing to do with them and, even though they failed to advise George or me, claimed they cleared the aircraft earlier that day, therefore relinquishing all responsibility.

The police denied all responsibility, stating a guard was initially posted on the aircraft at the direction of the air force and that the air force had instructed the guard's removal at 11.00am that morning.

Finally, beaten, tired and dejected, it got through to us that absolutely no one was going to take responsibility for Charlie Golf being ransacked and tampered with and there would be no compensation or replacement of our safety devices or equipment.

One particular safety device we carried with us was a relatively harmless, but very noisy starter pistol. Fortunately, George had the foresight to keep it with our personal gear at all times and so we were relieved that it had not been taken in the theft.

This fiasco left us feeling extremely vulnerable, depressed and isolated.

—

Sunday 25 August
Calcutta, India

We rose at 9.00am and immediately started preparing our statements for the Director General of Civil Aviation in Delhi and also for Mr Campbell. We delivered the completed and signed statement to Mr Campbell personally and then went for breakfast.

We had been told of a newspaper article that reflected on us negatively and asked the newsagent in the airport terminal if he could find us a copy. We picked up the newspaper and were dumbfounded and dismayed to read the following.

> **Amrita Bazar Patrika, Friday August 23 1968**
> *British Couple Get It All Wrong*
> *The Australian bonanza for Mr Wright and his wife seems now a long way off as both the husband and wife are detained in Calcutta for two days on a charge of violating the Indian aircraft rules and following an unconventional flight plan over India.*
>
> *Mr Wright's entry into India sparked suspicion the moment he flouted the request of the Civil Aviation*

Department to fly from Lahore to Delhi. Mr Wright and his wife, both of them British nationals and on their way as immigrants to Australia, wanted to fly in their Beagle Terrier plane from Karachi to Bhuj. Despite Government's objection they flew to Bhuj on August 3rd and landed in the soup.

Lot of explaining done, and after the intervention of the British High Commission in India the couple were allowed to leave Bhuj but were cautioned and asked to fly via Delhi — Lucknow — Banaras and Calcutta but Mr Wright violated this request too and flew following the Ahmedabad — Raipur — Ranchi road. His next troubles started when he made an unscheduled landing in Jamshedpur and made a touch and go landing in a restricted military airfield in West Bengal. Before he could be intercepted he flew to Dum Dum and landed here.

On top of his past records of unconventional flights in India Mr Wright has a lot of explaining to do to extricate himself of the jam; [sic] a justified demand from the Indian authorities for flying over the restricted zone involving leaks of security.

His Beagle Terrier under guard a real 'terrier' at Dum Dum, with armed guards snarling to anybody venturing to take a snap, unhappy Mr and Mrs Wright are busy filling numerous forms and filing statements to justify their case, while the promised land yet seems far away. If he continued the same practice, Mr Wright might find himself in greater trouble in the beleaguered South East Asia, than he was in India, commented a security officer on Thursday. 'In India it was just formalities elsewhere it may not be the same', he added.

Whereas some of it was factual, we believed the assumption that George purposefully violated rules and regulations and defined instructions to be a complete fabrication (in this instance anyway). As would be expected, George was not happy and tried unsuccessfully to contact the newspaper direct.

Our next task was to check with BOAC to see if the valve had arrived. Unfortunately, it hadn't, despite the fact that Mr Simmins claimed to have despatched it three days before.

It seemed another day of getting nowhere, so we wandered over to Charlie Golf to have another look at the damaged life jackets and to once again give the rest of the aircraft a thorough inspection. We were with Charlie Golf about five minutes when two customs officials came over to discuss the ransacking and theft. While George was showing them the damaged lifejackets, we all noticed that something had been stuffed into the lifejacket hood. When we pulled it free, lo and behold, it turned out to be some of the missing paper money from George's flying suit. For the second time that morning we were shocked, dumbfounded and confused.

We had no idea who would have done this or why.

Although thankful that some of the money had been returned, we were upset and appalled at the treatment we had received since landing in Calcutta that we decided from then on we would let things take their course and do and say nothing more until we were well out of the country. Only because it was necessary did we report our find to all the relevant departmental officials.

Interestingly, Mr Campbell's advice was to get the hell out of India before our problems escalated and we found ourselves in real danger.

We were badly shaken by this advice, so we lay low in our room the rest of the day.

I recall gazing out of the window watching the Qantas jet land and take off again and wishing so very badly that I was a passenger flying out of this bloody hell-hole. I was also terribly, terribly homesick and longed to see a friendly familiar face again.

—

Monday 26 August
Calcutta, India

There was a severe thunderstorm during the night and, as George's bed was beside the open window that could only be closed from the outside due to the flyscreen, he and his bed got soaked. We spent the rest of the night with the two of us squashed into one very narrow bed.

That morning the valve still hadn't arrived. It wasn't on the 2.00pm flight from London either.

In the afternoon, we met Guy Phillips in the cafeteria for coffee and he kindly invited us to have dinner with him and his family the following day.

After spending a very sociable hour with Guy, George was called to the telephone. On his return, I knew it was bad news by the look on his face. Apparently BOAC had sent a signal to the Beagle Terrier company enquiring the whereabouts of the radio valve and had been told that it was being despatched on 27 August. We should have expected to receive it in about seven days. This was after George had been told it was despatched on 23 August.

Once again, totally dejected, we returned to our meagre accommodation and read before retiring for the night.

—

Tuesday 27 August
Calcutta, India

I had nightmares during the night and when I woke my eyes were all puffy as if I had a cold.

While I spent the morning doing personal chores and writing up the diary, George tried to locate a radio and transmitter company called Marconi that he had been told was in Calcutta. He reasoned they may have a valve that suited our radio transmitter, therefore enabling us to leave Calcutta sooner than if we wait for the despatch from London.

The radio engineer from BOAC also tried to assist by checking out the set and, after looking up his charts, decided he couldn't be of any help.

Later in the afternoon, we took a taxi to Guy's home. This time we had no interference from the police.

It was so refreshing to find Guy, his wife Beulah, and children, Clayton and Gillian, to be a very down-to-earth, warm, loving family, living in a western-style, modest flat. We spent a very relaxing evening with them listening to his traditional jazz record collection and talking about our respective aspirations. We had just finished the evening meal when the power went off, so we spent the rest of the time with them in candlelight.

We learned that, as an airport customs officer, Guy was taking a huge risk in befriending us. He divulged that he was quietly making arrangements for him and his family to legally immigrate to Australia within the next twelve months. He told us that if his Indian colleagues knew of his plan, his career in the customs department would be jeopardised. He also told us that Anglo-Indians were not allowed to take any money whatsoever out of the country. As such, he was already secretly sending cash and saleable goods to Australia so that he had some available finances when he got there with the family.

George and I fully appreciated and were empathetic towards his interest in us and our trip and, as Guy had already decided to make his home in South Australia, his friendship was quite understandable. He was also quite embarrassed and apologetic about the treatment we had received from the various Indian government departments, the military and the police.

That night the Phillips family restored our faith in human nature and we vowed to help them all we could once we got to Australia. That is, of course, if we got to Australia.

Wednesday 28 August
Calcutta, India

I was woken from my nightmares by a persistent knocking on our guest room door. Apparently, George too was having nightmares and so when he answered the door he was not in the most congenial frame of mind.

Our morning visitor was Mr Campbell. He wanted us to sign a written statement declaring that we wished the police to immediately cease any action regarding the theft of our money. George, still bleary-eyed, told him we would call in to his office later to discuss the matter. According to Mr Campbell this wasn't an option, as his superior was demanding the statement in writing and without delay.

After discussing the matter over breakfast, George and I decided we would not sign any more statements and if this meant Mr Campbell would take the matter further, then so be it. George then walked over to Mr Campbell's office to advise him of our decision.

Later, while we were sitting out on the veranda reading, we

were interrupted by two uniformed police officers asking for statements. George spoke to them, then left to take them over to Charlie Golf to show them how, and from where, the money had been stolen and then, in part, returned. When George got back, he said that the officers had just been asking routine questions and had given an assurance that we would not be held at Calcutta Dum Dum any longer than we found it necessary.

By late afternoon, I had finished *Tale of Two Cities,* so before dinner we bought another couple of books. *The Robe* for me and *Dr Zhivago* for George.

I have never been good at lazing around with nothing constructive to occupy me. That day, I was so bored and running out of patience. I think we were both becoming stir-crazy with the inactivity and uncertainty of our immediate future.

With inactivity comes the inability to sleep. I'm afraid my foul mood and anxieties got the better of me that night and I was very rude and obnoxious to be with.

—

Thursday 29 August
Calcutta, India

Absolutely fed up with lounging around reading, that morning I wrote messages home on postcards until it was time for us to check with BOAC about the arrival of the radio transmitter valve. Much to our disappointment, there was no delivery, which meant another long agonising day of waiting.

When the weather cooled down later in the day, together we wandered over to Charlie Golf to turn over the engine and generally ensure all was well. All was not well. George noticed that with continually being exposed to the heat and the sun, the leading edge of the wings had bevelled in several places.

I think that was the last straw, as the two of us just went to pieces. It was all too much. Back in our room, we cried, raged, argued and generally "lost it". Through tears of frustration, we tried to justify the emotional cost with the pleasure and overall purpose for the trip.

Somewhere in the middle of all that, George went to see if he could buy a bottle of whisky somewhere. He couldn't.

I knew I had lost my resolve, so, while he was gone, I actually knelt and passionately prayed for strength, guidance and the will to continue. By the time George returned, I had taken control of myself again and, despite the frustration eating away at both of us, we were able to once more communicate in a calm and civil manner.

By 10.00pm, we showered and retired for the night, still feeling helpless, powerless and vulnerable.

Friday 30 August
Calcutta, India

George couldn't sleep, so he went for a walk in the middle of the night to break the boredom. I slept a little, but woke feeling chilled, as if I was fighting a virus.

At the appointed time, George called in at the BOAC office and came back to the room with the good news that at long last the replacement valve had arrived. He had to go back in about an hour's time to fill out the paperwork for clearance through customs for onward trans-shipment.

Feeling greatly relieved, I proceeded to air traffic control to send a signal to Chittagong advising of our anticipated arrival, file a flight plan and order a Met report.

My tasks completed, I joined George and a customs officer out on the tarmac. The precious valve was fitted into the radio under the direct supervision of the customs officer. We were unable to run an immediate check on the replacement valve as our headsets were back in the room at the guest house.

Feeling quite buoyant and somewhat surreal, we grabbed two iced Cokes at the airport terminal cafeteria and went back to our room to start preparations for an onward flight the next morning. At about 5.00pm, we made our way back to the aircraft with our headsets to check the radio and ensure the replacement valve was working.

Much to our dismay, we still couldn't get a response from the transmitter. Now what? George reasoned that Charlie Golf may be parked in a blind spot and decided to seek permission from air traffic control to move to another parking bay. He then got cold feet and thought it best to keep the problem to ourselves for the time being.

We had been asked to return to BOAC to fill in forms and collect cargo manifests. Feeling quite dejected, we made that our next stop.

It was so very hot and we were burdened with indecision as to what would be our best move, given the circumstances.

When all the packing and preparation was completed, we found ourselves reminiscing over our recent honeymoon in Northern Ireland and our warm-hearted Irish relatives.

Chapter 17

East Pakistan

In the air again and a friendly reception

Saturday 31 August 1968
Calcutta — Chittagong, East Pakistan
Time of departure: 00.13 GMT Flying time: 2hrs 22mins
Flying conditions: Hot, low cloud, mist Wind direction and velocity: 250°/10knots.

The end of August, after eleven days stuck in Calcutta, at long last we were able to resume our trip to Australia.

I rose immediately the alarm went off at 1.00am local time. Despite the fact that George had been vomiting, we ate a mild breakfast and gave ourselves plenty of time to conduct all the necessary tasks and paperwork and clear customs. Even so, we just managed to keep to our time frames as scheduled on the flight plan.

Guy came over to say farewell before we climbed into the cockpit. It was then that he told us that his work colleagues had sent a report to the Delhi Customs Office concerning his friendship with us. He also disclosed that the whole time we were in Calcutta we had been followed, albeit discreetly.

We thanked him sincerely for the risks he had taken and told him that we would do everything to help him and his family should they ever make it as far as Australia. In reality, Guy's tribulations were not greatly different from our own.

Once in the cockpit, we held our breaths as George attempted to raise air traffic control over the radio transmitter and failed. Bloody hell! Now what? George rolled Charlie Golf forward out of the parking bay and onto the apron. Success! We had good communication, that is, until we got to the end of the runway and then it cut out again.

After flashing the navigation lights to let air traffic control know that we could hear their signal, they gave us permission to roll forward and proceed with take-off.

We were airborne, we were relieved, and we were elated.

The flight to Chittagong was uneventful and very pleasant. Navigation was easy despite the poor visibility, and we located Chittagong Airport right on schedule. Once on the ground, it was gratifying to be greeted with genuine warmth and civility.

Our immediate task was to report to air traffic control to find out how to get permission to enter Burmese airspace. As we had suspected, clearance had to be sought through government channels and not civil aviation.

As such, and without delay, we contacted the British Trade Commission in Chittagong. Much to our joy, a Mr Tony Lovelock knew all about us and had been expecting us to contact them on 14 or 15 August as he already had clearance for us to travel through Burma on those dates.

I arranged with Mr Lovelock to go straight to his office as soon as we had cleared airport customs and immigration.

Clearing the airport did not take very long and, having decided to refuel Charlie Golf later, we climbed aboard a scooter taxi with all our baggage and asked to be taken into the city. Another rather cramped, but fun, experience.

The sights of Chittagong were pleasing to the eye. Large shipping vessels and small junks crowded the river. We were very conscious of the fact that we had no films to record the scenery and, quite frankly, having lost everything we had taken up to Calcutta, our enthusiasm for taking more photographs was non-existent.

Over tea in his office, Mr Lovelock and his colleagues helped us to plan the next few stages of our journey from East Pakistan into Burma. We were then taken to the Club House where we were to be housed. Here, we discovered that for very reasonable accommodation rates, we had access to a swimming pool, bar and a great deal of social activity. Our room had no shower or air conditioning, but we didn't mind at all. We were just so happy to be among friendly and trusting people.

Having unpacked and freshened up, we gravitated to the bar where we immediately made friends with a Mr and Mrs Shepherd, their family and friends. They invited us back to their home where we spent a pleasant afternoon socialising.

At about 4.00pm, Mr Lovelock returned with the news that we should send a postal telegram to the Burmese authorities in Rangoon post haste as the Burmese signals office was closed until Tuesday morning. He kindly drove us to the post office where we quickly despatched a telegram. Before dropping us back at the Club House, he very kindly invited us to dine with him and his wife the following evening.

Once back in our room, I knew that if I lay down I would sleep 'til morning, so I took the opportunity to write up the diary and send more postcards to loved ones back home. We were interrupted by a bearer who brought us a delicious pot of tea and then lit several slow-burning mosquito rings so that we did not have to use the nets. Such thoughtfulness and attention was heart-warming.

Back in the bar before dinner, we met up with a group of people from Scotland. They insisted we join them for a drink, although it was apparent one couple in particular had obviously had more than their fair share of drink already. My diary notes that the couple were in fact a Mr and Mrs Scotland.

We thought the couple were a bit rough and loud-mouthed, so when they invited us to a party at their house I didn't think George would accept; but he did. I was quite exhausted but didn't say anything as I didn't want to appear a party pooper. There were three or four young people at the gathering, but we didn't really enjoy ourselves as Mrs Scotland was dancing with the young men all the time and constantly loudly abusing her husband in front of the whole company. At about 1.30am, one of the older men in the group brought us back to our lodgings. George was quite drunk by this time and I was just relieved to get into bed to sleep.

—

Sunday 1 September
Chittagong, East Pakistan

We had ordered tea in our room for 9.00am, but either the bearer didn't come, or I didn't hear the knock on the door. Regardless I didn't rise 'til 11.00. While George still slept, I washed clothes and caught up with other personal and writing chores.

At 2.00pm, I thought George had slept long enough, so I woke him and the two of us went to the restaurant for lunch. On the way past the bar, we were ambushed by our drinking acquaintances of the previous evening. Once again, George accepted the invitation to join them for a drink and we ended up staying in the bar until it closed in the late afternoon.

I was starving and furious and it took a lot of self-control not to lose my temper. Once back in our room, George ordered sandwiches and coffee, but by this time I wanted to eat something much more substantial. As far as I was concerned, he had too much to drink and so another argument was inevitable. I decided to climb back into bed for a nap before we went out for the evening.

After a couple of hours of deep sleep, I woke at 7.00pm in time to get ready for the 7.45pm car that was to take us to Tony and Janet Lovelock's home. We had a fantastic social evening dining with this most hospitable couple and a few of their friends. At the end of the evening, one of the group, an Australian, dropped us back at the club guest house at 2.00am.

—

Monday 2 September
Chittagong, East Pakistan

At 8.00am, the bearer knocked on the door and I collected a tray of tea and bananas from him. We had been told that the club guest rooms were booked out for the next few nights, so we were quite pleased when George managed to book us in for that night. However, it did mean we would have to find alternative accommodation for the rest of our stay in Chittagong.

That day was spent much the same as many others, catching up on small chores, reading and writing. At 5.00pm, we ventured out to the new market of Chittagong, did some window shopping and purchased a few needy items. Feeling rather weary, we agreed to forego a dinner at the Chinese restaurant and made our way back to the club in another of the tiny taxi cabs.

Back in the club bar before dinner, we befriended another British national called Barry Cutthill. Barry was extremely friendly and very eager to help us in any way he could.

We managed to retire at 10.30, much earlier than we had done for the past few nights.

—

Tuesday 3 September
Chittagong, East Pakistan

Our wake-up call this morning was 9.15. With delight we learned that not only had our clearance to fly into Burma come through but we were also able to stay one more night at the club. As quickly as we could, we made our way to Tony Lovelock's office to collect the telegram and then found a bank to change money.

While George was dealing with bank issues, I took a local "baby" taxi to the airport to supervise the refuelling of Charlie Golf, order a Met report and file a flight plan to Cox's Bazar for the following day. I was informed that we would not be able to take off before 8.00am local time as the air traffic control staff didn't commence duty until that time.

During the afternoon, George sent a signal to Rangoon advising of our estimated time of departure from Chittagong and our estimated time of arrival into Burmese air space.

When we paid the guest house bill later that afternoon, we were invited into the secretary's office for drinks. After a pleasant hour spent discussing local issues and our experiences, we called in at the restaurant. Whole pigeon was the main dish on the menu that night. The diary notes do not indicate whether or not it was palatable, just that I was feeling slightly off-colour and had a mild asthma attack before going to bed.

—

Wednesday 4 September 1968
Chittagong – Cox's Bazar, East Pakistan

Time of departure: 02.01 GMT Flying time: 1hr 11mins
Flying conditions: Hot, low cloud, severe mist Wind direction and velocity: 90/°10knots.

Another night of broken sleep, and then of course I didn't hear the alarm at 5.00am. Fortunately, I stirred at 5.30 and got up feeling reasonably fresh.

Back on schedule at the airport, the officials processed our departure efficiently and we managed an 8.00am local time take-off. However, on the runway we did have another mag drop, but fortunately it cleared reasonably quickly.

This morning's flight to Cox's Bazar was uneventful until we entered Cox's Bazar air space. Cox's Bazar was surrounded in low cloud, rain and sea mist. George took to the coast in order to fly safely at a lower altitude, but even over the sea we were unable to squeeze under the cloud mass. We circled the area for a while and then at the first opportunity we slipped through a gap in the cloud and, despite a minor communication problem with the radio, landed safely on the airstrip at Cox's Bazar. By this time, the rain was coming down in torrents, but the welcome from airport staff was cordial.

Clearly, we would be unable to fly again in the afternoon, so we cancelled the onward flight plan to Akyab in Burma.

After changing money, we booked ourselves into a very moderate, but hugely expensive, beach guest house. Later in the afternoon, the skies cleared and I was able to take a long, luxuriously walk along the beach and paddle my feet at the water's edge. I love the sand and the sea, so this relaxing diversion did wonders for my battered soul.

Before dinner, we returned to Charlie Golf to check the spark plugs we thought might be causing the mag drop. To George's surprise, they were all clean and showed no signs of oiling up. We were joined by the airport manager and a few ground staff and together we tied Charlie Golf down for the night.

We returned to the guest house and dined on leathery, tasteless chicken before we turned in for the night ourselves.

Chapter 18

Burma

A perilous near-miss incident

Thursday 5 September

Cox's Bazar – Akyab, Burma

Time of departure: 02.20 GMT Flying time: 1hr 18mins

Flying conditions: Low cloud, stratus poor visibility. Wind direction and velocity: south-west-south.

When I woke at 5.30, I was disappointed to find the weather had closed in again. Regardless, we made the decision to chance our luck and try to get to Akyab that day; given it would be a reasonably short trip.

We had no problems departing Cox's Bazar, but the low cloud, rain and poor visibility did give us a few anxious moments. However, by flying between 500ft and 2000ft along the coast, we made it safely to Akyab.

It was a pleasant surprise to be met by efficient ground crew who immediately refuelled Charlie Golf before we even reported to air traffic control. In fact, all the airport formalities were completed quickly and efficiently.

The next leg of our trip to Rangoon was to be a long one at 300nautical miles, so, as a precautionary measure, we once again filled up the plastic container with avgas in case we experienced strong head winds on the way.

—

Akyab — Rangoon

Time of departure: 05.01 GMT Flying time: 4hrs 21mins
Flying conditions: Low cloud, thunderstorms. Wind direction and velocity: south-west-south.

At 11.30am local time, we were back in the skies heading for Rangoon. Because of the severe weather conditions, we again flew along the coast. However, even then, George was forced to drop to 500ft and below to get under the storm clouds. The good news was that at all times we were in radio contact with the airfields we were flying past or other aircraft flying overhead.

As we came into Rangoon airspace, the poor visibility hampered my ability to immediately locate the airport. Eventually, we spotted the runway lights and, although we'd just had the most exhausting trip for a while, George executed a perfect landing on a runway awash with water.

As we had now flown over 5,000nautical miles, it was always our plan to have Charlie Golf serviced in Rangoon by a company called Fairweather Smith & Co. Unbeknown to us, Fairweather Smith was no longer in business. This was rather a concern as Charlie Golf and the Gypsy Major engine were very much in need of attention. Unfortunately, there was nothing we could do about it but keep heading south and try to get the service done at another large airport.

In Rangoon, we had a slight problem with immigration as we were not in possession of traveller's visas. Issuing us with visas was not the concern. It was the fact that the officers were going to charge us treble the cost because they were on overtime hours. This was at 4.00pm in the afternoon. Harsh words were exchanged and eventually they promised to issue us with a twenty-four-hour visa for a nominal £2, but only when we supplied them with a passport type photograph.

A twenty-four-hour visa did not seem very long, but we decided not to raise this concern at the time.

Collecting our baggage, we made our way to the taxi rank with the intention of heading into the city for a night's accommodation. Before we could hail a taxi, we were approached by a very friendly Burmese gentleman, Reverend John Thetgui, who was apparently farewelling his American friends at the airport. We gratefully accepted his offer to take us into Rangoon.

While we waited for the Reverend, George produced a letter that had been given to him when he reported in to the flight briefing room. The precious letter was from my mum and dad and had been addressed c/o Rangoon Airport.

I was totally overcome and wept tears of joy to have news of family and friends at home and to know we had not been forgotten. George too was smiling with joy.

Feeling overwhelmed and elated, we rode into Rangoon in the back of our new friend's car. Reverend Thetgui and his wife took us to a photographer to have passport/visa photos taken. This was followed up with a meal at a Chinese restaurant.

While we were having dinner, we learned that Reverend Thetgui and his wife were Christians working for the Burmese Christian Society in Rangoon. His wife was a teacher. After a very filling meal, this warm and hospitable couple took us to their home. Their home was quaint, cosy and completely made of wood. Here, we sat in the comfort of their kitchen, talked and drank coffee, while John took lots of photographs of us. His son then drove us to the Christian guest house where we were to spend the night. Reverend Thetgui kindly offered to return to Rangoon to collect our visa photographs.

As if these lovely people hadn't done enough for us, they promised to collect us from the guest house the following morning and deliver us to the airport.

Before going to bed, I prepared for the next day's flight and wrote up the diary. I was so happy. It had been a wonderful day.

—

Friday 6 September
Rangoon — Moulmein, Burma

Time of departure: 03.27 GMT   Flying time: 4hrs 07mins
Flying conditions: Rain and thunderstorms. Wind direction and velocity: south-west.

Unfortunately, that morning, I woke with a very bad head cold and puffy, sticky eyes. Regardless, we got ready for a day's flying and met Reverend Thetgui and his wife for breakfast at 6.30am. As promised, he gave us our visa photographs.

It was over breakfast that our host disclosed that he didn't know how much longer he would be able to stay in Burma because the new communist Burmese Government was forcing missionaries of all denominations, and particularly the Americans, out of the country.

Back at the airport, Reverend John Thetgui took many more photographs of us as we said our goodbyes.

While collecting a Met report and filing our flight plan, air traffic control sent cables to Bangkok and Butterworth for onward clearance on our behalf. The cables were very costly, but we didn't mind.

Our next task was to clear customs and health. We waited for what seemed like ages at the Immigration Department desk, but no-one was around, so we left the visa photographs with one of the bearers to give to the officer as soon as he arrived.

We had just climbed into Charlie Golf, when George was requested to report immediately to air traffic control. He was told we had to be out of Burmese air space by 4.00pm local time that same day. We smiled at each other and shrugged. There was no way Charlie Golf could travel that distance in that space of time. We had scheduled ourselves at least one more fuel stop in Burma before we flew into Thailand. This time we knew we would be breaking the rules. However, we had absolutely no other choice but to keep going south and hope to hell we weren't intercepted or arrested.

Having been given the appropriate clearance, we took off for Tavoy, our next scheduled stop.

We were only airborne five minutes, when air traffic control came over the radio transmitter telling us to return to Rangoon and clear immigration. George was furious and unsuccessfully tried to persuade the authorities to let us continue the flight.

Back at Rangoon airport, we parked Charlie Golf on the apron and very grudgingly filled out and signed two forms for the immigration official. We then hurriedly left, climbed aboard Charlie Golf and took off for the second time that morning.

By this time it was 10.00am local time and the weather had worsened and flying conditions were extremely hazardous.

As we were straining to maintain visual contact with the coastline on our left, George suddenly yanked the joystick and veered dangerously to the right. I yelled out as it was so unexpected. Then, as we skirted round a large grey shape, the reason for his action became obvious. George had seen the grey mass looming ominously through the mist and suddenly realised it was a tall outcrop of solid rock. There is absolutely no doubt that his vigilance and quick action saved our lives that day.

About sixty nautical miles out of Tavoy, we just couldn't get through the worsening cloud cover and so, having decided we'd had enough near misses for the day, turned back to Moulmein, our chosen alternative airstrip.

Running very low on fuel, we made a reasonable landing in Moulmein. We were immediately greeted by the entire town of people who stood around and watched with fascination as Charlie Golf was refuelled. Moulmein was a very small place.

Before being taken into the town by the airstrip's government representative, we did a few small running repairs to Charlie Golf's canvas skin, then secured the aircraft for the rest of our stay. Because of the severe weather, there was no hope of an onward flight that day.

The Government Rest House, our accommodation for the night, was quite different to anything we had stayed in before. The diary notes describe it as being dingy and foreboding on the outside, standing on stilts about four feet off the ground. The front veranda was shaped like a threepenny bit and had stairs leading up from both sides. The interior was a long, wide corridor with black, wooden, double doors leading from it. Our room had bare floor boards with gaps between the slats through which you could see daylight. There were two hard, wooden beds, a round table and several wooden chairs. The whole effect gave a cool, comfortable feel and it was very clean. I also noted that Burmese women are so tiny, petite and pretty.

We had cold drinks and biscuits, followed by a cold shower and then bed for an early night. The beds were so hard that George decided to crawl in beside me. In the middle of the night I was wheezing and coughing and so uncomfortable that I took my pillow and climbed onto George's vacant bed to sleep.

—

Saturday 7 September
Moulmein–Mergui, Burma

Time of departure: 02.20 GMT   Flying time: 3hrs 43mins
Flying conditions: Occasional thunderstorm, poor visibility.
Wind direction and velocity: 250°/12knots.

Everything we owned was damp when we woke due to the

constant rain and extreme humidity. To add to my discomfort, my cold seemed worse and my eyes were puffy and glued shut. Nevertheless, I bathed them open and tried to forget about the other symptoms of my cold.

When we turned up at the airport, we were told that the en-route weather was forecast as low cloud, heavy rain and more thunderstorms. Extremely conscious of the fact that we were supposed to be out of Burma by now, George decided we would wait at the airport for an hour or so in the hope that the weather would clear enough to enable us to fly.

At around 8.30am a Fokker Friendship flying overhead between Tavoy and Rangoon reported that the weather had improved and was not too severe. That did it. George decided we would get underway and attempt to fly at least as far as Tavoy. We reasoned that the further away from Rangoon we were, the better and safer we would be.

By 9.00am, we were airborne. Initially, we had to dodge under and around the rainstorms, but the nearer we got to Tavoy, the better the weather became. As such, we continued our journey on to Mergui without dropping in to Tavoy.

We made Mergui in good time, but, unfortunately, once we were there the landing was not so pretty. To get out of Burma as quickly as we could we considered flying on to Phuket in Thailand that afternoon. However, when we ordered a Met report, we were informed that we could expect very heavy rain and thunderstorms with *cumulus nimbus*. We decided to stay put and do an overnight stay in Mergui.

Charlie Golf's tanks duly filled with avgas, we were taken to the Strand Hotel. Like other Burmese buildings, the Strand was built of wood. On the first floor small cubicles came off each side of a wide, central hallway. Our cubicle, number 3, contained two beds, one table and one wardrobe. Apart from a wall-to-wall mosquito net, the ceiling was open to the main hallway. The one window in our cubicle looked over the tin roof of the adjacent building, but behind that there was a tree laden with coconuts.

The rather smelly shoreline of Mergui was lined with other wooden houses, shacks and fishing boats.

All the while we were taking in the sights, sounds and smells of the town, we were accompanied by a crowd of very friendly curious onlookers all of whom were dressed in their native, batik fabric clothes.

That night, the log book and diary having been updated, we dined on soup and very tasty fried rice. We had hoped for a good night's rest, but that wasn't to be as we were woken at around midnight by the pounding rain and the howling of the local dogs.

Chapter 19

Thailand

A multicultural wedding and pristine beaches

Sunday 8 September 1968
Mergui–Phuket, Thailand
Time of departure: 00.55 GMT Flying time: 3hrs 52mins
Flying conditions: Rainstorms, fair visibility, turbulence.
Wind direction and velocity: 260°/15knots.

More discomfort for me when I woke. My hands and arms were covered with mosquito bites. George had none.

We paid a very high price for our Mergui overnight stay, about four times that of our stay in Rangoon for less comfortable accommodation. Having no choice, George reluctantly paid the bill.

The weather in Mergui was cloudy, dark and overcast and getting an accurate Met report from the airport traffic controllers wasn't easy as it had to come from the Rangoon Met office. This morning, the Rangoon Met office forecast high cloud with the occasional thunderstorm. Considering the conditions we had managed to negotiate over the past four or five days, we felt reasonably confident that we could get Charlie Golf safely through to Phuket.

Before we were allowed to leave, the Burmese customs officer demanded a large sum of Burmese currency from us for having to work on a Sunday. George was not prepared to open his wallet again, so told the officer that the hotel had taken all our money and we had none left to give him. The officer reluctantly allowed us to leave Mergui.

Although turbulent, our flight to Phuket was pleasant and much more relaxed than those of the past week. The visibility was fair and allowed us to enjoy the magnificent scenery of the Burmese, Thailand, coastline. The sea was different shades of blue and green, the beaches appeared sandy and pristine and the lagoons were a shimmering brilliance.

The day got even better. Firstly, it was a great relief to be clear of Burmese air space and secondly, when we landed in Phuket, we found the airport terminal to be modern and most certainly westernised.

Because it was Sunday, the Esso fuel representative couldn't refuel Charlie Golf, plus he needed to confirm with his office in Bangkok that he could accept our fuel carnet. This meant we were unable to continue on to Bangkok. Somehow, it didn't seem too much of a problem that day as everything else had gone right for us.

After satisfying the authorities at the airport that we were healthy, trustworthy bona-fida travellers, we took a taxi into Phuket and booked into a rather flashy hotel with air conditioning and showers in the rooms.

So far, we were pleased to encounter nothing but happy welcoming smiles from all the personnel with whom we came in contact.

Once ensconced in our luxury surroundings, I washed all our clothes and brought the paperwork up to date while George disappeared to change money. As was our usual habit when we had freshened up ourselves, we went down to the hotel bar for a cold beer.

At the next table from us there was a group of easily identifiable

Europeans who asked us if we cared to join them. We found ourselves in the company of a Glasgow couple who, by chance, were to be married on Wednesday; an Australian couple, an Australian from Kuala Lumpur; and an Australian who was married to a Thai woman. When we joined their table, it was clear they had been celebrating for quite some time and by this time we too were feeling the effects of alcohol on an empty stomach.

More drinking ensued. At some point in the late afternoon, it was agreed that George and I would stay in Phuket with Lea and Frank Ashton, the Australian couple, until the wedding on Wednesday. We would then fly to Kuala Lumpur on Thursday and stay with Alan Munro, the Australian working in Malaysia, who would also be flying out on that day.

To us this seemed a most welcome distraction and a great chance to get to know some real Australians.

All the arrangements agreed upon, we left to go to Frank and Lea's house for more drinks and hors d'oeuvres. We were all in a party mood and while the men drank Lea took me upstairs to look for something I could wear to the wedding. By the time we re-joined the men, George had far too much to drink and so Frank and Alan drove us back to the hotel where George went straight to bed and conked out.

I still hadn't had a proper meal, so Alan and I went down to the restaurant and dined on shark's fin soup. I wasn't particularly impressed with the soup, but was willing to try anything once. Alan and I sat and talked until the waiters turned us out at 9.30pm.

There was a large, sulphur-crested cockatoo in the hotel bar, which, earlier in the afternoon, had taken a chunk out of George's finger. That bite must have turned septic, as George said it was very painful and took ages to heal.

—

Monday 9 September
Phuket, Thailand

We got out of bed as soon as the alarm sounded. George went out to the shops to get himself some cigarettes and change money, while I packed the cases and made ready to move to Frank and Lea Ashton's house.

While George returned to the airport to fuel up Charlie Golf and make known our intended movements over the next week, Lea and I went to Lea's friend, Barbara's, house to see if she had something suitable I could wear to the wedding. No luck with the wardrobe, but we did have fun chatting over coffee with yet another two of her friends. On the way back to Lea's house, we collected George, Frank and Alan from the hotel bar.

After a delicious cold meat salad lunch, George and I decided to go into Phuket to see the sights. We bought a photograph album to give to the bride and groom as a wedding gift.

We spent the rest of the day in the company of Frank, Alan and Lea socialising and enjoying the marvellous food prepared by Lea's 'cookie'.

Relaxed and pleasantly weary, we took ourselves off to bed at 10.00pm.

—

Tuesday 10 September
Phuket, Thailand

It was another agreeable day, warm and sunny with some cloud.

George and Alan had arranged to look round the tin smelting works for the morning while I popped back to Barbara's to talk dresses again. Eventually, I decided to wear my own mini dress and, as the fashion had not yet reached this part of the world, hoped no-one would be offended.

Next stop for Lea and I was the grocer's and then to the market where Lea bought a piece of jewellery for Alan to give to the bride. I looked longingly at a stunning princess ring studded with many different coloured stones, but it was far too expensive for our budget.

After another delicious lunch of noodles, prawns, egg and salad, followed by homemade ice cream, Lea and I found time to call in at the church to see to the wedding decorations. Later that night, we all went to the club to see the movie *Khartoum*. That was a fun night as the picture kept sticking and jumping. Regardless, it kept us amused and we all enjoyed the movie.

When George and I returned to our room that night, laid out waiting for us was a supper of rolls and apple pie. We were overcome with gratitude for the superb hospitality and friendliness shown by this couple and their friends.

—

Wednesday 11 September
Phuket, Thailand

It was the day of the wedding and the weather was warm with sunny spells.

In the morning, we were lucky to get the services of Suma, one of the drivers. In a brand new, pale green Holden with cream leather bench seats, we were chauffeured to a beach surrounded by lush tropical greenery and coconut palms. I was ecstatic. We meandered along deep sand, pristine, clear, blue-green sea with white breakers throwing up a cool spray. I was rather sad I couldn't go for a swim, but the tide was in flood and the undercurrent too strong. Nevertheless, we still paddled and splashed around in the shallows. We got very wet and took a lot of movie film. These movie films never turned out.

Feeling relaxed and content, we asked the driver to take us back to the Ashton's so that we could get ready for the wedding.

The wedding itself was an interesting "mish-mash" of cultures. The wedding couple, Mary and John, were Scottish. The best man was Australian married to a Thai. The officiating Church of England minister was Malaysian. The lesson was read in English, then in Thai by a Thai Catholic priest. The hymns were sung in English by a congregation of mainly Thai speaking nationals. All in all, it was a joyous and uplifting experience.

After the service, everyone congregated at the Ashton's house for the reception. There the spread of food was unbelievable, with roast lamb, roast pork, chickens, and large platters of gigantic prawns.

The bride and groom left the gathering in the traditional way, that is, in a car decorated with tin cans, buckets and toilet paper.

George and I felt quite fortunate to have been asked to share a wonderful day with such hospitable and generous people.

Chapter 20

Malaysia

Thursday 12 September 1968
Phuket–Penang, Malaysia
Time of departure: 03.05 GMT Flying time: 3hrs 08mins
Flying conditions: Warm, few clouds fair visibility. Wind direction and velocity: 260°/15knots.

It was time to say goodbye to our hosts and get back to the job of flying to Australia in a single-engine aircraft. We were both feeling quite buoyant and confident when we rose at 7.00am.

At 8.30, we boarded Frank's dormy van and en-route to the airport we picked up a couple of customs and immigration officers.

Alan and the bride and groom were also at the airport waiting for their flight to Penang via Sonkla.

After haggling the cost of landing and parking fees, we took off from Phuket at 10.00am local time. Before setting a heading for Penang, George took Charlie Golf over to Frank and Lea's home where we circled for a few minutes and waggled the wings.

Our journey to Penang flying at 3000ft was delightful as we enjoyed the good weather and splendid scenery the country had to offer.

Butterfield, the nearby military base, had us on radar and we were requested to circle overhead to allow another flight to land in Penang, Georgetown.

As soon as we touched down in Penang, we were met by Alan Munro who had arrived only minutes before us. While we were talking with Alan, we were paged and instructed to report to air traffic control. Once there, we received a dressing down for not reporting to them immediately we landed. We just couldn't win. Everyone wanted a piece of us at the same time.

Our next hop that day would be a short one, so George arranged to have only Charlie Golf's belly tank refuelled.

We enjoyed a lunch of fried rice in the cafeteria with Alan before making our way back to Charlie Golf and preparing for our second flight of the day.

During lunch we learned that Mary and John, the bridal couple, had been refused entry into Penang and sent back to Phuket because John's passport was not in order. George and I fully empathised with their situation as it would not have been the best start to a honeymoon.

—

Thursday 12 September
Penang–Kuala Lumpur, Malaysia

Time of departure: 07.49 GMT Flying time: 2hrs 27mins
Flying conditions: Hot, clear sky, haze, poor visibility. Wind direction and velocity: 260°/15knots.

We greatly appreciated the experience of good weather flying again and the flight to Kuala Lumpur was no exception. The trip was uneventful despite the haze causing poor visibility.

As we entered Kuala Lumpur airspace, air traffic control instructed us to approach from the south and land on runway 33. As this meant we had a tail wind, George requested that we land into the wind on the alternative runway. George was told that Kuala Lumpur airport only had one runway! George didn't argue the point and expertly brought Charlie Golf in to land despite the strong tail wind.

We found the new airport at Kuala Lumpur to be quite spectacular and impressive.

As we hoped to get the much needed and overdue service done on Charlie Golf's engine while we were in Kuala Lumpur, we did not bother about refuelling the tanks; instead, we gathered up our gear and made for the luxurious looking terminal building complex.

Alan appeared while our passports were being stamped. His flight had again preceded ours by only minutes.

By the time we were settled in Alan's very comfortable bungalow in Kuala Lumpur, it was night-fall and after such a busy day we watched television while we had supper. The three of us then turned in for the night.

—

Friday 13 September
Kuala Lumpur, Malaysia

Being Friday the 13th, perhaps it was fortunate we had no plans to fly.

Given Charlie Golf had completed over 120 flying hours and covered just over 8,000 nautical miles, our priority of the day was to arrange to have the aircraft fully serviced. Alan had already offered to contact a member of the local flying club who could advise us on the maintenance for Charlie Golf.

In the early afternoon, we accompanied Alan to the offices of the Straits Times Newspaper where we were interviewed by a female reporter. Alan went back to his office while George and I returned to the airport with the media entourage to have photographs taken beside Charlie Golf.

While at the airport, George called in to one of the

engineering companies to enquire about aircraft servicing and maintenance. The manager was not available, but George had been asked to take the log books back to the office the following day. This sounded quite promising and we had high expectations that we would get the work done here before resuming our journey.

That evening, Alan had another commitment; however, he arranged for us to have dinner with a young New Zealand couple, Anna and Brian. At 8.00pm a car came to take us to their very beautiful, modern home.

We were delighted to discover that Anna and Brian were of our own age and with a similar outlook on life. We connected immediately.

After a dinner of minestrone soup and pasta, Brian fitted George out with one of his shirts and a tie and the three of us left to meet Alan and some more of his friends at a night club. The remainder of the evening was spent exchanging hilarious stories and generally having a really good laugh.

—

Saturday 14 September
Kuala Lumpur, Malaysia

Kam, Alan's housekeeper woke me at 7.00am and it was with great difficulty that I roused George. As I suspected, the effect of the alcohol consumed the evening before had not yet worn off.

After dropping Alan at his office, the driver took George and me to the engineering company's hangar at Kuala Lumpur airport. There, we were extremely disappointed to be informed that they were much too busy to handle the work on Charlie Golf. It was suggested we wait until we reached Singapore and have it done there.

Rather dejected, we made the decision to leave for Singapore first thing on Monday morning as the air-worthiness of our aircraft was becoming a critical issue we needed to have resolved.

Later that morning, we dropped in at the large shopping complex in Kuala Lumpur city and were delighted to find a Marks and Spencer store. I was overjoyed at being able to replenish much needed underwear and other personal items. We window shopped for a while and then, just like we would have done back in Glasgow, we stopped in at a cafeteria for a decent cup of coffee.

That evening, we were to be Alan's guests at a ladies' dinner at the Masonic Lodge, so in order to look and feel our best, a sleep in the afternoon seemed like a good strategy.

At 7.00pm, dressed in our finery, we drove to the Masonic Hall where we met up with Anna, Brian and "Legs". Legs was yet another friend of Alan's who, as well as being quite a flamboyant character, also had artificial legs, hence the name.

The photographs taken during the function depict a most attractive blond, Anna, with a fashionable hair style and cool, floral, summer dress, and Alan, Brian and Legs in dinner suits and bow ties.

That evening turned out to be a very enjoyable experience for George and I. Each lady was presented with a gift. I received a small pewter vase etched with traditional Malay symbols. George was lucky enough to win 200 cigarettes. The formal meal was delicious and, as always, the alcohol was flowing freely.

During the evening, we were fortunate to be introduced to the Malaysian Defence Minister who kindly promised to look into the problem we were having getting Charlie Golf serviced to air-worthiness standards.

Alan, George and I were almost the last to leave at 2.00am.

—

Sunday 15 September
Kuala Lumpur, Malaysia

Feeling quite groggy and hung-over, I eventually crawled out of bed at 10.00am. George didn't surface 'til almost lunchtime.

Speaking with Alan, I learned that he had been busy on the telephone most of the morning in an attempt to contact members of the Flying Club who might have been able to help us. He had also had a telephone call from a Group Captain of the Air Force. Apparently the Defence Minister had contacted him earlier that morning.

Early in the afternoon at the Flying Club, we met Ted Baille-Reynolds, a very influential member. Ted's advice was to forget about having work done on Charlie Golf in Kuala Lumpur and to wait until we got to Singapore. Much to our surprise, Ted also gave us a twelve-gallon capacity, ARB (Aircraft Registration Board) approved, aluminium tank that he had used on a similar aircraft to the Beagle Terrier. There was a possibility we could get the tank fitted to the rear seat mountings while in Singapore. The extra fuel it held would give us a range of six-and-a-half hours, which would be an enormous advantage through Indonesia.

Ted also indicated he could possibly supply us with a different pitched propeller that would give Charlie Golf better lift and greater air speed. It was agreed George would telephone him the following day with propeller dimensions and model numbers.

The next stop off for the day was back at the Club with Alan where we were introduced to yet more of his buddies. Here lunch and drinks were on "Gus" as it was his birthday. George and I had oysters, followed by steak, egg and chips.

We finished the day back at Alan's home with supper and an early night in bed.

—

Monday 16 September
Kuala Lumpur, Malaysia

It was Monday morning and we were still gratefully appreciating the hospitality of Alan Munro in Kuala Lumpur.

We lazed away the morning doing chores, then after lunch I went off to spend the afternoon with Anna, while George returned to the airport to have Charlie Golf refuelled and to file a flight plan for Tuesday's trip to Singapore. Anna and I spent a cherished afternoon together chatting and doing simple, homely things like baking passionfruit pie and making sandwiches.

Anna and Brian arranged to take George and me out to dinner for our last evening in Kuala Lumpur and so at 8.00pm they collected us from Alan's home and we made our way to the most sumptuous and luxurious Lake Club.

The four of us had a brilliant evening at this quiet, intimate venue. The band played soft background music as we enjoyed each other's company as well as the oysters, caviar and T-bone steaks with all the trimmings.

Much too soon the evening came to a close and we exchanged sad and tearful farewells with our cherished friends.

Later, as I packed our gear for the onward journey, I had a very heavy heart. We had met so many generous people and said so many goodbyes over the last three months.

Dining at the Masonic Ladies' Night — Kuala Lumpur
L-R Anna, George and Brian

Auld Lang Syne *at the Masonic Ladies' Night*
L-R Alan, "Legs", George and Brian

Chapter 21

Singapore

A relationship in jeopardy and Charlie Golf's air-worthiness service

Tuesday 17 September 1968

Kuala Lumpur – Singapore, Singapore

Time of departure: 02.27 GMT Flying time: 2hrs 24mins

Flying conditions: Cool, cloudy, good visibility. Wind direction and velocity: 260°/15knots.

At 6.30am local time, we arose to another day of saying goodbye and flying on to our next destination. During the night the weather had changed to torrential downpours, but this morning the front had weakened and left us with high clouds.

We farewelled Alan at his office and Kam drove us to the airport. First off we left our gear with Kam while we collected our weather report from the Met office and then reported to air traffic control. Our next task was to clear immigration, health and customs. Our formalities completed, we left Kam looking somewhat sad in the terminal.

Once more in the cockpit of Charlie Golf, George started the engine and, on instruction, taxied forward across the apron waiting for permission to roll forward for take-off. Almost immediately, air traffic control came on the radio telling us that a Mr Munro wanted to talk with us urgently. Confused as to what it could be about, we returned Charlie Golf to the parking bay and shut down the engine.

When we caught up with Alan in the terminal building, he had come to tell us that the Group Captain who had been approached by the Minister of Defence had rung him enquiring if there was anything more he could do to help us. We were overwhelmed to think that Alan had rushed from his office to the airport to give us the message. We thanked him profusely, but stuck with our decision to head for Singapore and get the work done there.

Once in the air, our flight to Singapore was plain sailing, although George was kept extremely busy with the constant radio transmission demands. Clearly, we were approaching a very busy and crowded airspace, but the additional vigilance kept us from getting bored.

Unfortunately at such a busy international airport as Singapore, George's landing was not the best as he came down rather hard and bounced on the runway. At least we didn't loop the loop.

After parking and reporting to the necessary authorities, we made straight for the Flying Club.

Here we spoke with Mr Fry, the Flying Club gentleman responsible for aircraft maintenance. After listening to our plight, he told us to move Charlie Golf to the Flying Club hangar and leave the log books on his desk. We were crossing our fingers hoping that we would at last get an air-worthiness check done on our Beagle Terrier aircraft.

With high hopes, we stripped the aircraft of all our paraphernalia and cleaned out all the odd bits of rubbish collected on the way. Our gear went in to storage for safe keeping.

Before taking a taxi into Singapore city, I checked to see if any mail from Scotland had been forwarded to the airport for our collection. I was disappointed when told there was none.

The hotel recommended by the taxi driver was The Strand. We found it to be reasonable and comfortable and so booked ourselves in. After a beer at the hotel bar, we wandered down the street to find the main shopping area. Later in the afternoon, George managed to locate a street map and guide to the city.

During our evening meanderings, we came across a young couple doing chalk drawings on the pavement outside a cinema. Written beside the drawings were the words, *We are trying to get to Australia in a sampan but our engine has broken — any help would be appreciated.*

Naturally, we got talking to the pair and learned that the girl was Australian and the boy was a New Zealander. They, with their six companions, were living and travelling on a sampan. The water pump had broken down and was in the process of being repaired. Although they were roughing it, there was nothing George or I could do to help them and, besides, looking at the amount of donations already in their collection box, they could probably have helped us.

George and I did a little more sightseeing, then had a quick meal in the Chinese restaurant opposite the hotel before returning to our room and bed.

—

Wednesday 18 September
Singapore

We knew we would be grounded in Singapore for at least the next few days, so this morning we thought it would be a lot easier if we had our own wheels. We discovered that car rentals were not too expensive and so hired a white Morris Minor. It was a bit rough round the paintwork and upholstery, but quite adequate for our purposes.

Enjoying our new-found freedom and independence, we drove

ourselves back to the Flying Club and spoke with Mr Fry about the work that was required to be done on Charlie Golf. Within a very short space of time, the Beagle Terrier had been washed down and the canvas skin inspected for faults or damage.

Comfortable with the knowledge that the maintenance of Charlie Golf was in good hands, we decided to maximise our use of the Morris and went for a drive along the east coast 'til we reached Changi. Although there were some good swimming spots on the beaches, we didn't venture into the water. Instead, we looked round the village of Changi, did some window shopping and bought postcards.

I drove the car back to the hotel and, having been driven around by taxi drivers, chauffeurs and friends for the past three months, it was good to know I could still change gears.

That evening, we were supposed to collect official forms from one of the Flying Club officers. However, he was apparently caught up in a meeting. Rather than hang around waiting, and as it was getting late, we ventured back into the bright lights of Singapore to find somewhere to eat.

The first place we tried was a Chinese restaurant and bar, a cool, gloomy place with strong-smelling incense. As soon as we found a seat and ordered beers, we realised something was not quite what it had first seemed. It quickly became apparent that as soon as a male person came into the premises, he was immediately joined by one of the many tall hostesses sitting at the bar. None of the girls left the establishment and those sitting with a man appeared to be receiving money for exchanging small talk. We decided against ordering a meal in the establishment and quickly left.

At our second choice of restaurant, we were rudely informed that it was too late to serve meals, but it was quite apparent that this place was conducting a business similar to that of the one we had just left.

By this time we gave up and, instead, had a late dinner at the Chinese restaurant opposite the Strand Hotel.

—

Thursday 19 September
Singapore

First thing in the morning, George received a telephone call from a foreign correspondent named Mr Wise who worked for the British tabloid, *Sunday Mirror,* asking if we would meet him at the Singapore Flying Club at 1.00pm. We cordially agreed to his request.

Being the retail utopia of the world, George and I decided it was time to go shopping in the city. We looked around for a radio, a man's Navi-timer watch and wooden Scholl sandals for me, to name just a few items on the most wanted list. George priced a Swiss Brethiung Navi-timer, but it was extremely expensive and it was missing the instruction book. He was sorely tempted to buy, but decided to wait until the instruction book could be included in the purchase. We told the salesperson we would return another day. We hunted for a few of the other items on our list, but without much success.

By this time, it was nearing 1.00pm, so we headed for the airport. For the umpteenth time we got lost in the traffic on the way there. Mr Wise and his wife were waiting for us at the bar, but as they had other business to attend to first, we agreed to meet again later.

George and I took the opportunity to check up on the progress of Charlie Golf and to see if we had any mail from the U.K.

I was overjoyed when told I could collect a letter from the Office of Apron Control.

This five-week-old letter was also from my parents, but with much the same news and contents as the first. Apparently, my father had assumed we did not receive the letter he sent to Rangoon and so had sent another one to the British High Commission in Singapore, who in turn forwarded it to the airport. Regardless, it was an enormous boost to our spirits to receive mail and know we were in our families' thoughts.

When we again met up with Mr and Mrs Wise, he elected to take us to lunch at the Goodwood Club in the city. The Goodwood Club was very luxurious and costly, but apparently Mr Wise was using his business account that day so no expense was spared. We dined on smoked salmon and fillet steaks prior to submitting to endless questions about our en-route experiences.

During lunch, Mr Wise had recommended cheaper accommodation in Changi. George and I decided we would drive out to investigate the Casuarinas Hotel that had been recommended to us. When we got there, the proprietor was unavailable, but we spoke to an English family who were staying there and over tea and scones we learned that the food was good and the prices very reasonable.

Later, when Margaret, the proprietor, arrived, she immediately recognised us from local newspaper articles and offered us full board for two at a special, cheap rate with all meals included. She said we could move in on Monday. She also told us she could get us a much cheaper deal for car rental.

Back at the Strand Hotel, I wrote postcards and brought the diary up to date before climbing into bed at 1.30am.

—

Friday 20 September
Singapore

That morning, I bought underwear, a jumper and perfume and posted twenty-six postcards to family and friends. George was still undecided about the chronometer, but after he'd read the instructions and haggled with the salesperson, he finally relented and made the purchase.

Feeling rather guilty about spending so much money, we settled on a trip to the Changi RAF base to see if we could beg or borrow maps of Indonesia that were more up to date than the ones we were working with.

We made inquiries with both the RAF Survival School and the Operations Room and were grateful to be issued with not only decent topographical maps, but also a new edition of the radio frequency book. While in the company of very knowledgeable experts, I enquired as to the prevailing winds over the Timor Sea and what we might expect at this time of the year. We learned that for the Timor crossing, we could expect headwinds, although they would be very light. We left the RAF base in good spirits.

At 3.00pm, we were back at the flying club admiring Charlie Golf's touch-up respray. The Beagle Terrier was looking quite smart again. We were also advised that the ARB representative had received a response from London regarding the carrying out of the Certificate of Airworthiness and that he had been given the authority to take the matter into his own hands.

By 4.00pm, we were back in the flying club bar being interviewed by a Mr Barker for an article to be published in the next edition of the flying club's magazine and also for the local newspapers.

While at the club, we were approached by one of the members who was considering flying his own aircraft back to U.K. in two or three weeks' time. He was eager to talk to us, so invited us to have dinner with him the following evening.

By the time we left the flying club, and feeling the effects of the alcohol, we felt a meal of fish and chips out of a newspaper was quite in order. Following directions given to us in the bar, we found the fish shop easily and then drove down a quiet side street and, just like we would have done back in Glasgow, ate our fish suppers while sitting in the car, We really enjoyed that meal.

Back at the hotel and feeling quite confident about our travels, we spread the newly acquired maps on the floor and worked out the most appropriate route to take through Indonesia before crossing the Timor Sea into Darwin.

—

Saturday 21 September
Singapore

That morning, we reasoned it was time to explore how to obtain permission to enter Indonesian and Portuguese Timor air space. With this in mind, we called in on the British Embassy. Here we were told that the Embassy was unable to assist as it did not have an Air Attaché. Instead, we were advised to contact the Indonesian Air Attaché in Djakarta.

I drafted a letter and completed the given forms to post to Indonesia. We also tried to locate the Portuguese Consulate with a view to obtaining permission to fly into Baucau, but we were unable to locate its office.

With these tasks completed and the black clouds of an incoming storm not far away, we decided to take a break, head to Changi beach and watch the weather roll in over the sea. We drove the car slowly along the seafront watching the strong wind bend and sway the palm trees and whip up a spray of white foam off the sea.

In Changi village, we bought hot bread, sardines, meat paste, doughnuts and fruit, then drove back along the beach to find a place to picnic and possibly swim once the storm abated.

Later, we returned to the Casuarinas Hotel and whiled away

the remainder of the afternoon in the bar, drinking and reading old magazines.

At some point, George decided he wanted to go to Johore. We got lost again and the usual bitter quarrel ensued as George lost patience and became angry. Eventually, in uncomfortable silence, we came upon signposts indicating the direction to Johore. We came upon the border so suddenly that George had to do a quick U-turn and retrace our steps in order not to become involved with customs officers.

Unbelievably, we got lost again trying to find our way back to our Singapore hotel and by this time tempers were really flying.

When we eventually got back, George decided he wanted to go out for a drink, but as I was sick of the drinking routine, he went alone while I busied myself with chores. On his return, he told me he had enjoyed several beers in the company of a hostess in the bar we had the misfortune to happen upon earlier in the week.

I didn't know what to think. I felt confused, lonely and dreadfully unhappy, but I had no alternative but accept the situation I found myself in. I reasoned I must be doing something wrong, but I couldn't figure out what it was or even how to fix it, so I did nothing except take myself to bed.

Sunday 22 September
Singapore

After the troubles of the previous evening, neither of us got out of bed 'til very late. During the night I was plagued with strange dreams of people back home and that left me emotionally drained and depressed.

At around lunchtime, we went back to Changi and the Casuarinas Hotel with the intentions of going for a swim. However, we didn't get that far as we were asked to join a young Singapore couple at the bar. Here, an elderly friend of theirs was buying the drinks.

I again tired of the bar routine, so I took myself back to where the car was parked and lay on the grass in the sun for a while. By this time the tide had gone out, so I was unable to have a swim. I had been sunbaking for only a short while when I started to feel very queasy. I made my way to the change rooms and, by the time I got there, my head was spinning and my legs had turned to jelly. I tried taking a cold shower, but had to hang onto the door handle to stay upright. After finding a stool and sitting with my head between my knees, I felt strong enough to dress and return to the bar where George and his friend were. When I explained what had happened, I was given a cup of black tea and gradually I started to feel better.

George then drove me back to the Strand Hotel and left me in the room while he went out for another drink and something for us to eat. An hour later, he came back drunk and with no food.

We tried to discuss our problems, but didn't get very far. I was getting increasingly frustrated and angry, while George seemed unable to rationalise or reason through his inebriated state.

At 10.00pm, he left, saying he was going for a drive to clear his mind.

I ordered an iced Coke and read for a while. I must have fallen asleep because when I woke it was 2.20am and George hadn't returned. I was beside myself with worry and wondering what to do, when he finally arrived at 3.00am. He was still drunk and his mood was just as bad as when he left.

His explanations of the nocturnal wanderings didn't make sense and seemed somewhat far-fetched. Needless to say, I couldn't sleep, so took pen and paper and wrote all my feelings down just as if I was talking to someone. This must have helped as the diary indicates I managed to get a few hours' sleep.

—

Monday 23 September
Singapore

We rose at 9.00 and, with the weather warmer and the atmosphere decidedly cooler, I packed up all our gear in readiness for moving to the Casuarinas Hotel while George settled the Strand Hotel bill.

On the way to our new accommodation, we paid a visit to the Flying Club to catch up with Mr Fry and to check on Charlie Golf. Mr Fry handed the log books back to George telling him to contact the ARB representative in the administration building of the airport. However, George was told to call back the next day as the account had not been finalised.

While driving to the Casuarinas Hotel, I raised the issue of the previous night's arguments. The ensuing heated discussion seemed to be going nowhere, so I took the attitude that there was no point in thinking about it anymore as there was nothing I could do in the present circumstances. I resolved to deal with it another time. After all, I had made the commitment that we started as a team and therefore we would finish as a team.

Once settled into room number one at the Casuarinas Hotel, we lazed around in the sun and swam until late afternoon.

It was as we were getting ready to go to dinner at Col Baillie's home (we met Col Baillie earlier in Kuala Lumpur) that the first cockroach appeared. I happened to move a waste basket to one side and out from underneath ran the biggest, ugliest, shiny black cockroach I had ever seen. I jumped. Then two or three more scuttled across the floor. I was horrified. Cockroaches seemed to be everywhere. We quickly moved our case, bags and shoes up off the floor.

Later, when we spoke to Margaret, it was apparent that cockroaches were a fact of life at the hotel and the best tactic was to ignore them. Ugh!.

We spent the evening pleasantly socialising with Col Baillie and his navigator, Squadron Leader Key. We were surprised to learn that the two of them would be flying their own aircraft back to U.K. and on the way intended to stop off to see Stanford and Judy Howard in Karachi.

George and I were both in good spirits by the time we left and so stopped off for fish and chips on the way back to the Casuarinas Hotel.

—

Tuesday 24 September
Singapore

Feeling somewhat lethargic, we spent the best part of the day swimming, reading and generally lazing around.

In the late afternoon, while watching Margaret, the proprietor, and her friend play Scrabble, the reporter from the *Straits Times* arrived to interview us and to take some photographs. On leaving, we were told that the article would probably be published in the *Malaya Mail* the following afternoon. When I look back at the photographs taken that evening, I can see my mouth is smiling but there is sadness in my eyes.

Margaret then called us over to admire the cheap car she had procured for us to rent. It was an old banger of an ancient, soft-top Morris Minor, side valve model. The hood didn't sit on the body of the car, a shock absorber was defunct, the rear lamp unit was broken and the front near side light wasn't working. It was a heap, but a cheap heap.

We enjoyed an evening meal of roast duck and then played Scrabble with the others for the rest of the night. There was plenty of exuberance playing Scrabble and we all had a really good laugh.

—

Wednesday 25 September
Singapore

That day we had a few loose ends to tie up and errands to run.

The first job was to empty the first hired car and return it to the rental company. Next was to go back to the Strand Hotel and pick up George's pyjamas that he'd left in the room the previous day.

We then had another try at locating the Portuguese Embassy, only to discover that their premises had closed down and we would have to contact the Hong Kong branch.

The watch George had purchased a few days earlier was playing up, so we returned to the shop and left the watch to be repaired. It was fixed and returned to us within half an hour.

Our last port of call was to the Singapore Flying Club, where we were delighted to see Charlie Golf looking quite splendid, even though the engine was still to be assembled. We were told the Beagle Terrier had been given a thorough check and, apart from the brakes and an engine mounting, no serious faults had been found.

Mr Fry then informed us that the cost of the overhaul was approximately Singapore $500 or £75. This was really good news as we expected a much more costly bill.

In the afternoon, we were asked to visit the local school and give a short talk to the children. We agreed and scheduled a time for the following Monday.

That evening, after another game of Scrabble with Margaret

and the other hotel patrons, I checked the Clearance and Frequency book and discovered that no prior permission was required to enter Portuguese air space. As such, we had no reason to contact the Portuguese Embassy in Hong Kong.

—

Thursday 26 September
Singapore

The weather that morning had turned nasty and I felt a cold coming on.

Regardless, as arranged, we headed out to the RAF Base to meet Squadron Leader Key. For security reasons, we were held at the main gate until Squadron Leader Key arrived. We were then escorted on a tour of the base and introduced to the officers of 205 Squadron. As part of the tour we were shown around the cockpit of a Shackleton aircraft which we found to be extremely interesting.

While at the base, Squadron Leader Key managed to scrounge a flying suit for George and have our life jackets that had been tampered with checked for damage.

The rest of the afternoon was spent socialising in the officers' mess.

Once back at the Casuarinas Hotel, we were pleased to find the air conditioner in our room was now working efficiently, so we spent the rest of the evening lazing around watching television and playing Scrabble.

—

Friday 27 September
Singapore

We woke to more bad weather and George suffering with a cold. To occupy ourselves, we wandered across to the shopping complex and purchased a few small personal items and then decided to drive the old Morris banger out to the flying club.

At the club, we were heartened to see Charlie Golf was almost in one piece again, apart from the fitting of the new tank. We were also pleased to receive a letter from the Air Attaché in Indonesia informing us that we should very soon receive clearance to fly into Indonesian air space. This was great news to digest.

That night was spent in much the same way as the past few and we were beginning to get restless and bored.

—

Saturday 28 September
Singapore

During the previous evening, we had made up our mind to relieve Charlie Golf of some of the unnecessary weight by sending the used topographical maps and other redundant baggage to my brother, David, in Australia.

With this in mind, we returned to the Changi shopping complex to buy pewter napkin rings and pewter tankards to add to the parcel. I was hoping to buy fabric, but didn't find any at a price that made it worthwhile to post.

That evening we had the pleasure of watching a beautiful moonflower come into bloom, giving off the most exotic aroma. We were told that, according to folklore, it is very lucky to see the moonflower open.

—

Sunday 29 September
Singapore

We seemed to have been in Singapore forever and it was getting tiresome.

That day, being Sunday, we accompanied two other hotel patrons, John and Florence, into the Peoples' Park market in Singapore. There, I bought four lengths of printed Thai cotton and as John and Florence successfully haggled with the stall owners, my purchase price was most reasonable.

Leaving the market, John took us for a drive to the highest point on the Singapore peninsula from where we could look over the bay at the ships and across the peninsula at the airport.

We then took John and Florence to the flying club to show them Charlie Golf. While at the club, I was very happy to be given a newly arrived letter from George's mum. We had great pleasure reading all the latest news from Scotland while returning to the hotel in the back seat of John's car.

Before retiring for the evening, we carefully packed the maps, pewter items and fabric in a large box ready to post to David the following morning.

—

Monday 30 September
Singapore

By 10.00am, we were outside the Casuarinas Hotel waiting for the taxi to take us to the Changi Infant School. At the school, we were met by the headmistress, Miss Simpson, and duly shown around the junior classes before having morning tea with the staff in the staff room. This was followed by an assembly of the older children who sang a couple of hymns and performed a short play about Noah. George and I visited several classrooms and spoke to the children of some of our en-route experiences. I told them of the Yerdla Children's Home in India run by the Reverend Court and suggested the children might like to write to the Reverend with a view to corresponding with the children in the Home. Finally, we were presented with a gift of a small pewter glass stand. Before we left, we were also introduced to the headmaster of the Junior School and it was agreed we might visit the school, depending on the length of our stay in Singapore.

In the afternoon, we took the parcel we had boxed up the previous night to the post office in Changi, only to be told that it was too heavy to go by mail. Our options were to send it by shipping freight or split the contents and make two parcels. We decided on the latter.

My next task was to write to Reverend Court telling him of our school visit that morning and advising him that he may get letters from the children of the Changi Infant School.

—

Tuesday 1 October
Singapore

October already and we were still stuck in Singapore with a severe thunderstorm brewing.

I recalled waking during the night feeling excited and enthused as I realised we would shortly be resuming our journey to Australia and now Australia didn't seem that far away.

With nothing much else to do that morning, I caught up with a few chores and updated the diary.

George decided to go to the China Sea Beach Club with a guy called Teo. I did not like this person, and neither did the other hotel guests, but George still went.

He got back after lunch and it was quite obvious he had far too much to drink again, so the atmosphere between us was very strained.

For want of something to occupy us, we decided to return to the airport to see if there was any more mail for us and to find out how Charlie Golf's maintenance was coming along.

George criticised my driving the whole way out to the airport, so much so that by the time we got there I was a nervous wreck.

We removed the aircraft's rear seat made redundant by the installation of the extra fuel tank and took it to a pilot who had earlier agreed to take it with him to Darwin free of charge. We were to collect the seat when we arrived in Darwin on receipt of a letter proving ownership.

I flatly refused to drive us back to the hotel. This only served to increase George's anger and so another blazing argument ensued. I was so sick of the drink affecting George's moods and judgement that the rest of the day was spent in an atmosphere that could only be described as strained and extremely icy.

—

Wednesday 2 October
Singapore

After a very lazy morning, I went for a drive in the car on my own to pick up a few things from the shops. It was a hazardous trip as the brakes on the old banger were practically non-existent.

In the afternoon, Margaret invited us to go to a club and a Malaysian folk dancing show in the evening with herself and some of her friends. We gratefully accepted the invitation and by 7.00pm we were all dressed up and enjoying a drink in the bar with Margaret while we waited on the arrival of the others. When they arrived, we piled into two cars and made our way to the Villa Scuyana.

Villa Scuyana was situated by the sea, miles from the nearest village, and was operated by a bachelor who lived in a house in the surrounding gardens. These spectacular gardens consisted of palm trees, masses of fragrant flowers, coloured paving, paths and steps, and fountains with coloured lights. The stage with surrounding tables already set for dinner was arranged on a wooden jetty jutting out over the sea. This was also decorated with water features and palms and flowers all illuminated with coloured lights.

On arrival, Margaret introduced us to the proprietor. We were then shown to our table seating and presented with a delightful cocktail *aperitif* served in a half coconut shell decorated with flowers.

Our immediate company was RAF personnel and their wives, while the other one hundred or so patrons appeared to be mainly American and Australian.

Following the *aperitif*, each guest was given a colourful paper fan and invited to the buffet to partake of the entree. The men in our company brought Malaysian satay sticks and sauces to our table. We were then invited to congregate in the dining hall where we served ourselves with a choice of rice, fried rice, curry and many other exotic Asian dishes. Each guest was then served with a huge steak and a glass of wine. The feast finished with coffee.

When we returned to the jetty, we found the chairs had been arranged round the stage. Once everyone was settled in their seats, we were entertained by graceful Malayan folk dancers adorned in splendid, colourful costumes, followed by an exhibition of the art of Malayan self-defence. Two boys, in particular, put a great deal of energy into their performance and one cut his foot when he tumbled and fell onto a table of drinks. The final item was a humorous mock-up of Malayan wedding customs.

Afterwards, the audience was invited to take to the floor and join in the dancing. The entire show was excellent, entertaining and greatly enjoyed by all.

At the conclusion, our small party stayed behind and chatted with the proprietor. We learned that he owned a cabin cruiser, two cars (one of which was a Jaguar), a magnificent home and three cocker spaniels.

At the end of the evening and back in our room, we agreed that the entertainment was by far the most exotic and pleasurable experience of our trip.

—

Thursday 3 October
Singapore

After such a glorious evening, we slept in and did without breakfast. With nothing else to do, we whiled away the morning reading magazines and watching the rain streaming down the windows.

Directly after lunch, Margaret told us that she understood from the news report at 1.30pm that as from today, no aircraft would be allowed to refuel in Indonesia. We were flabbergasted. George immediately telephoned our contacts in the RAF while Margaret sought information from the notorieties of her acquaintances in the flying business.

Eventually, following several hours of grave concern, we learned the facts. Apparently, the real story was that no British RAF aircraft was allowed to refuel in the Philippines. What a relief!

After that drama, George and I took the car out in the pouring rain with the intention of calling in at the Flying Club. George was driving. We hadn't gone far when the brakes of the junk heap failed completely. In order to avoid running up the back of the van in front, George swerved over to the wrong side of the road, almost forcing two taxis into a ditch. With that, we carefully returned to the hotel and arranged to have the brakes fixed.

Much later that evening, a group of us ventured out to the Singapore Hotel night club to watch the cabaret and generally socialise. The men in our company were particularly awestruck by a stripper who had the ability to manipulate her body into unbelievably suggestive, and sometimes grotesque, positions.

It was early morning before we eventually got back to the hotel and into bed.

—

Friday 4 October
Singapore

Another sleep-in with no breakfast and I'm beginning to think we will never get out of Singapore.

That day we were pleased to learn that Charlie Golf, now back in one piece, was to be flight-tested tomorrow. Unfortunately, we had no clearance to fly into Indonesian air space as yet.

At the Flying Club, we spent time with two representatives from the Beagle Terrier company who were en-route delivering an aircraft to Tokyo.

We stayed in the hotel the rest of the day as the weather was still overcast and wet.

—

Saturday 5 October
Singapore

First thing in the morning, George went out to the Flying Club to watch Charlie Golf's test flight. He came back with the excellent news that the test flight was a success and the Beagle Terrier was in good order. For good measure, George also arranged to have the compass re-swung.

However, still no word from Indonesia. Tired of waiting around, we resolved to investigate if there was any way we could speed up the process.

That afternoon we had tea with Miss Simpson and agreed to visit the Seletar RAF Infant School the following Monday.

The remainder of the day was spent watching television and playing Scrabble with Margaret and the other patrons.

—

Sunday 6 October
Singapore

For a change, we rose to a hot, sunny day, so in the morning we wasted away our time on the beach swimming and sunbathing. Unfortunately, George, being fair skinned, got badly sunburnt again.

Apart from television and the occasional game of Scrabble, the rest of the day was spent in hours of inactivity and utter boredom.

—

Monday 7 October
Singapore

After an early start and a quick breakfast, we set out to find the Indonesian Embassy in Singapore. This was easier said than done, given that the streets were all one way. With the usual wrong turnings, lane jumping and a shouting match, we eventually located the embassy.

Once inside, we were sent from one enquiry desk to another and passed from person to person. This at least gave us a chance to appreciate the magnificent architecture of the building as well as the plush red carpets, marble staircase, fish tanks and lush gardens.

Finally, we were told the officer who deals with flight clearances was not available until the afternoon and we were given telephone numbers to contact him later in the day.

Our next task was to get from the embassy to the Seletar Infant School by 10.30am. Our luck was in as we managed to find our way through the maze of streets and arrive on time.

Once there, we were greeted by the deputy headmistress and fortified with a much needed drink of orange before being ushered into the assembly hall where about fifty children were gathered.

I proceeded to give my usual talk using the world map as a prop and relating some of our adventures en-route, while George fielded most of the questions. This was followed by morning coffee in the staff room with the teachers.

We were then taken to meet Mr Hodgson, the headmaster of the junior and senior schools. There, we moved from classroom to classroom, meeting pupils and answering more questions. As we left, we felt quite satisfied with our morning's work.

Later in the day, George telephoned the relevant officer in the Indonesian Embassy, only to be told that he could not be of any assistance and that George himself must contact the authorities in Djakarta. We immediately went to the post office to send a reply-paid telegram. This cost an exorbitant amount of money, but we reasoned it was worth it to speed up the clearance and get us out of Singapore.

The strain of the constant arguments with George and every other official we had to deal with was finally taking its toll on me and I was unable to sleep, so in the middle of the night I got up and went for a walk to clear my head.

—

Tuesday 8 October
Singapore

It was to be another day on the merry-go-round of red tape and bureaucracy.

First task that morning was to touch base with Mr Fry regarding the account for the Certificate of Airworthiness for Charlie Golf. While at the airport, we sorted through all the unwanted gear from our luggage. We then called in to air traffic control in the administration building to see if by chance our clearance had been sent to them, only to be faced with another disappointment.

Next stop was the 5th floor of the Aircraft Registration Board. As the officer dealing with our issues was busy, it was suggested we call him back in the afternoon. We left Paya Lebar Airport in rather a depressed state.

Back at the hotel, I was asked to take a telephone call from the RAF operations in Changi. I was totally overwhelmed when given the news that a signal giving us clearance to enter Indonesian air space had arrived at their office.

George and I were elated. We could now begin preparing for our long awaited departure.

After a celebratory beer and lunch, George took off to collect the signal. It indicated that we might have to fly to Kupang instead of Maumere, but we decided to deal with that deviation when we got to Djakarta.

Later, back at the airport, the officer in charge of maintenance at the Aircraft Registration Board told us that Charlie Golf's Certificate of Airworthiness was valid for another twelve months and would cost £2 to issue. We gasped at the price, but willingly paid up. We arranged to collect the log books from the Flying Club the following day.

From there, we called in to air traffic control and then to the Met office for a Thursday dawn forecast. We were told to telephone back the evening before we left as very often thunderstorms built up in the early morning. We were also provided with an airways map.

At about 5.00pm, we returned to the hotel where I was asked to take yet another telephone call. This time, it was from one of the school teachers whose fiancée was an officer in the RAF and flew through Indonesia regularly. They offered to come over and give us information and advice regarding the flying conditions we could expect to encounter. In reality, he didn't give us any new information, but we still found his advice worthwhile.

I managed to write a few more letters home to the U.K. and one to David in Australia giving them the good news that we would be on our way once more.

—

Wednesday 9 October
Singapore

After a good night's sleep, we rose immediately with a real sense of purpose.

We needed to stock up on personal items before leaving Singapore and so shopping was first on the list. En-route back to the Casuarinas Hotel, we took five minutes to watch two RAF helicopters undertaking manoeuvres and lowering an airman into the undergrowth on the end of a long wire or rope.

Back at the hotel, my job was to get clothes washed, dried and packed, while George went off to the Flying Club and airport to pay the bills and get Charlie Golf ready to resume our travels at first light. While there, he was told that our out-of-date fuel carnet could not be renewed before Friday and so we decided we would leave without it, as long as we had plenty of ready cash on hand.

We also settled our accounts with Margaret, who was extremely generous in giving us a worthwhile discount.

That night we were given a small farewell party by the hotel patrons with whom we had spent so much time and many games of Scrabble.

George and I retired to Room 1 for the last time at 9.00pm, although neither of us slept very well because of the anticipation of flying again.

Weary travellers on the Singapore tarmac

Playing Scrabble *to pass the time — Casuarinas Hotel, Singapore*

Chapter 22

Indonesia

A spectacular landing over a grass hut

Thursday 10 October 1968

Singapore–Palembang, Sumatra, Indonesia

Time of departure: 23.00 GMT Flying time: 3hrs 45mins
Flying conditions: Isolated thunder showers, poor visibility.
Wind direction and velocity: east/5knots.

After three tumultuous weeks in Singapore, we were finally leaving and eager to be on our way.

So when the alarm went off at 2.00am local time, we jumped out of bed and made ready in record time. As we left our room, we discovered the residents of the hotel sitting at the table playing Scrabble while waiting to see us off. John and Florence had arranged to drive us to the airport and those final goodbyes turned out to be quite emotional.

The six customs officers sitting round the table playing cards weren't the least bit interested in any paperwork or a declaration, so we took our gear straight over to Charlie Golf to load up.

When we opened the cockpit doors, we could smell avgas. On investigation, George discovered that the fuel pipe to the newly fitted tank was sweating and the open/shut switch did not move freely. George was far from happy, but we decided to push on regardless. Then George happened to mention that Charlie Golf might have trouble lifting off the ground because of the extra weight. That did put my nerves on edge. Not a good start to the day's flying.

With a bit of time to spare, we calmed our nerves with a coffee in the airport cafeteria before waking the immigration officer to give him the declaration form. I then filed the flight plan and collected the Met report. The forecast of isolated, thundery showers and *cumulus nimbus* was not ideal, but within acceptable limits for our purposes.

The sun was rising just as we got back to Charlie Golf, so we hastened our pre-flight safety procedures and called in for taxi clearance. To our utter amazement and delight, reliable old Charlie Golf lifted off the runway without any trouble at all.

I must have lost my touch because I was in trouble right from the start. We were unexpectedly instructed to report over a specific beacon. This threw out my prepared radio transmitter frequencies and, even though I was given the beacon co-ordinates, my mind went completely blank and I had real trouble working them out.

Sensibility kicked in; we duly reported over the beacon and were soon on our set course for Palembang.

Although we skirted the occasional storm, the three-hour flight was uneventful until we entered Palembang air space. Our occasional radio problems were still with us and we were unable to make contact with Palembang air traffic control. We circled the airport several times while trying the two frequency channels given in the RAF book, but to no avail. Then, as luck would have it, while we were messing about with the frequencies, we happened to pick up on .5 of a decimal off the lower frequency. Having at last established radio contact, we were brought in to land; however, the landing itself was rather sloppy.

The oil company refuelled Charlie Golf immediately we had

cleared customs, immigration and health, and we also managed to grab a drink before we took off again for Djakarta.

—

Palembang –Djakarta, Java

Time of departure: 03.49 GMT Flying time: 3hrs 14mins
Flying conditions: Hot, clear skies, good visibility. Wind direction and velocity: east/5knots.

What luxury, two trips in one day.

Our journey to Djakarta was also uneventful. Whereas in the morning we were flying over virgin jungle, the afternoon flight was mainly over water. Navigation was "spot on" and we made excellent time. On approach to Djakarta, we had no repeat of the radio problems and George made a perfect landing onto the designated runway.

On the ground again, George organised the refuelling procedure while I accompanied the customs officer back to the terminal building. Initially, he would not accept our general declaration and demanded to have it on a proper printed form. When told I didn't have one, he promptly informed me I would have to buy one from Garuda, the Indonesian airlines. I replied that I believed it was the customs' responsibility to supply the correct forms and, as the declaration I had provided was internationally acceptable, I had no intentions of forking out money for another piece of paper. The customs officer appeared to accept this and I was then escorted to the airport manager's office where our clearance papers were duly questioned. The manager stated that as he had not been informed of our intended arrival, he would keep the clearance papers overnight. It was also agreed that I would pay the airport fees first thing the following morning.

I was then escorted to the immigration officer's desk where

I retrieved our passports. Meanwhile, the customs officials had typed up their own copies of the declaration forms.

In Singapore, we had been warned that the Indonesian customs officers were liable to keep those items of your belongings that they took a fancy to, but for us this was not the case. We were ushered straight through the customs' check point by the same minder who had accompanied me through the immigration procedures.

Before leaving the airport, George tried to contact the Air Attaché in the British Embassy to find out the availability of fuel for our onward flight. He was told that the Attaché would not be back at his office until the following day. He also inquired about the cost of accommodation in Djakarta and was shocked when he learned how much we could expect to pay.

George made the decision that for the first time this trip, we would sleep the night in Charlie Golf.

All this time, our minder was still keeping a watchful eye on us.

The availability of fuel was still very much on our mind when we refreshed ourselves in the bar with a beer.

Back at air traffic control, George was told that there was no fuel available at Mau Mek or Sambawa. However, there was fuel at Bali. We then took our plight to the Garuda office and were told much the same thing. By this time, George got the strong impression he was being given the proverbial bum's rush.

Our only hope now was to plead with those in the Garuda head office to sell us some of their fuel at the airfields we would be passing through.

To add to George's discomfort and foul mood, he had been struggling with an extremely painful gum and toothache since we set out that morning and it was not getting any better.

We spent the next hour in the airport bar pondering over the maps and finally decided on another route that included only one airfield at which we would be required to purchase fuel from Garuda — the new route being Surabaja, Bali, Waingapu and on to Dili.

Neither of us could finish the meal we ordered in the restaurant. For me, the rice was too peppery, and, for George, his aching mouth was giving him too much pain to enable him to eat. As we were commiserating over our half-eaten dishes, an Australian joined us and asked if he could be of any assistance as he could tell we obviously had a problem.

Much to our surprise, he said he worked for an oil company and handed us the telephone number of a person he thought might be able to help us. We were extremely grateful.

After thanking him profusely, we grabbed our gear and wandered out onto the tarmac for a night's rest. The cockpit of Charlie Golf was much too cramped for two people, so I grabbed the lightweight 'chute, wrapped myself in it and settled down to sleep on the ground under the belly of the aircraft. About an hour later, the airport police woke me and told me I was not permitted to sleep on the tarmac. So it was back into the terminal building where we were allowed to sleep on the chairs in the customs hall.

Tired, cranky and covered in mosquito bites, we eventually succumbed to sleep.

—

Friday 11 October
Djakarta–Surabaja, Indonesia

Time of departure: 01.02 GMT Flying time: 5hrs 09mins
Flying conditions: Excellent, sunny with partial cloud cover.
Wind direction and velocity: east/5-10knots.

We woke with the dawn and I immediately locked myself in the ladies' room for a much needed wash and freshening up.

George's concerns were still fixed on the availability of fuel, so as soon as practical he paid another visit to the Garuda office. He came back with the good news that we could get fuel from Garuda Airlines in Waingapu without any trouble.

As the sun was rising and getting hotter, we quickly packed our gear into Charlie Golf and, while George went to change money, I went to Flight Briefing to file a flight plan and seek clearance to continue our journey.

After a slight delay while the officer checked with the manager's office, I was finally handed clearance papers. Then, when I was asked to pay the airport fees, the usual disagreements kicked in.

In the discourse that followed I quickly ascertained that:

- Surabaja, our next destination, most probably would not receive notification of our flight plan, nor of our intention to land at their airfield;
- should we happen to go missing between Djakarta and Surabaja, no search and rescue would be activated; and
- these conditions would prevail during all our flights in Indonesian air space.

As such, apart from the accepted landing fee, I could see no reason as to why we were being asked to pay such high fees that purportedly included the cost of search and rescue. After all, it was quite clear that no one would come looking for us in the event that we fail to arrive at our next destination.

The officer still demanded full payment in US dollars. I told him I had no US dollars, only Indonesian currency. He wouldn't accept Indonesian currency. I told him it was that or nothing and then went back to see the manager in his office. There, an angry exchange took place between three other officials and myself. I was told the aircraft would be impounded if I could not pay them US $8.

I marched over to the bank, slapped down all I had in Indonesian currency and asked for it to be changed into US dollars. I was given US $7. I then returned to the manager's office, gave him US $7 and told him it was all I had. To my surprise, he accepted it and gave me a receipt. I strongly suspected I had been taken for a sucker.

By this time, George was waiting in Charlie Golf, so I quickly ran across the apron in my bare feet and jumped in beside him. In no time we were airborne and on our way to Surabaja.

The first section of the flight was simple to navigate as it was a case of following the coast. However, when we turned inland, navigating was much more difficult as we encountered low cloud and very poor visibility. Nevertheless, Surabaja Juanda airfield came up right on target and we were given a straight-in approach.

George found it impossible to relax and enjoy his flying as he was still suffering from a very painful mouth.

Once on the ground, we were anxious to have Charlie Golf refuelled and to file another flight plan to Bali Denpasar.

Again, we had problems when it came to paying the airport fees. The airport officials once again demanded US $10. Again, we refused to pay that much. The refuelling procedure was then held up until we paid. We counteracted by explaining that we were not part of the commercial airlines and that we were embarking only on an internal flight, not an international one. This strategy appeared to work and they finally accepted the value of US $5 in their own currency, approximately two thousand Indonesian rupiahs. Interestingly, Juanda was the only airfield we had encountered that was staffed mainly by women who appeared to be part of the military. It was unclear whether army or air force.

Before taking off for Bali Denpasar, George bought several bottles of orange juice to sustain us on the way.

—

Surabaja–Bali Denpasar

Time of departure: 07.45 GMT Flying time: 2hrs 30mins
Flying conditions: Fair, with some rain storms. Wind direction and velocity: east/5-10knots.

After the five-hour trip from Djakarta to Surabaja in the first part of the day, we were fairly comfortable in the knowledge that we would be in the air for less than three hours during the heat of the afternoon.

This proved to be another very enjoyable trip as the scenery was quite magnificent.

A short distance out from Denpasar, we flew under a heavy rainstorm. We were fascinated to see a perfect rainbow encircle Charlie Golf and then, when we burst out from under the cloud, our entire surroundings took on the most remarkable blue tinges. It was quite breathtaking.

As we entered Bali Denpasar air space, we thought our radio transmitter problems had returned as we were unable to make radio contact with the air traffic control. George circled the tower three times and was given a green light enabling us to land. Unbelievably, we were given an apology and informed that their radio transmission system was faulty and currently undergoing technical repairs.

By the time Charlie Golf was being refuelled, it was dark, so we wasted no time in looking for a taxi. As seems to be the custom that as soon as we landed we were allocated an escort, or agent, as he was called, and it was he who instructed the driver to take us to the immigration offices in Bali. The officers on duty tried to persuade us that we required another visa, which, of course, would come at a cost. As we already possessed a valid visa, we argued the case and eventually won. Our appointed agent then took us to a reasonably priced hotel and arranged to collect us at 5.30am the following morning.

After washing away the day's grime and sweat, we left the hotel to do some sightseeing around Bali. We were somewhat disappointed and came to the conclusion that the tourist destination in 1968 was overrated. We would have liked to have seen more of the township round Denpasar as our first impression was that it had real local character.

George's mouth was still giving him a great deal of pain and so, after a very ordinary evening meal, he took Aspirins and went straight to bed.

I stayed up to catch up on the paperwork and could see that he was very restless and not sleeping well.

—

Saturday 12 October
Denpasar–Waingapu

Time of departure: 00.05 GMT Flying time: 5hrs 08mins
Flying conditions: Fair, strong cross wind on runway. Wind direction and velocity: n/a.

George was up half the night dealing with his pain, so it was no surprise that we overslept in the morning until 5.30am local time.

We dressed quickly and managed to get a coffee by the time our escort arrived to take us to the airport.

Once there, the self-appointed escort asked an exorbitant amount of money for his services. George paid him much less in his own currency and we could tell he was not at all happy about it.

After filing our flight plan, we were given clearance papers to travel to Waingapu, then asked to pay US $2. George tried a long shot and told the officer he must be mistaken as we were undertaking an internal flight and therefore no charge should apply. It worked and we didn't have to pay.

The flight to Waingapu was mainly over water. However; despite the non-availability of a Met report, navigation was made easy by the numerous islands along the route. Even that early in the morning, the sun was hot and we had to dodge a few black clouds.

The island we were heading for came into view just when it should, but as soon as our route left the sea and took us over the undulating land, the strong updraughts took effect and Charlie Golf bounced around like a cork on the water.

We quickly located the airstrip that was Waingapu. There was a 50ft drop into a river at one end of the landing strip, high rolling hills at the other and down each side mature trees stood like soldiers on parade. The strip itself was covered in high, thick grass and it was impossible to determine the condition of the landing surface.

As if the situation couldn't be worse, the wind sock was blowing constantly at 90° from its pole, which meant Charlie Golf would have to land in an extremely strong crosswind.

George carefully brought the aircraft in on the final run, but, with the strong crosswind, the up-currents and the surrounding terrain, Charlie Golf continued to bounce around and yawed dangerously with one wing in the air and the other skimming across the grass. The stall warning was screaming out at us. My heart was in my mouth.

George brought Charlie Golf round for a second try, hoping the crosswind would ease up, but the second attempt was more precarious than the first. The wind just swept Charlie Golf sideways. By this time we were both getting extremely anxious and there was a crowd of locals standing round the grass hut airstrip terminal watching our every move.

George shouted for me to find an alternative airstrip. Our old topographical map indicated there were two abandoned airstrips further along the coast, so we headed in that direction, but found them almost impossible to locate. We eventually flew over what we thought might once have been landing strips, but the terrain was so rough and unkempt that George rated them as too dangerous to use. However, he did identify another piece of land where we could put Charlie Golf down as a last resort should the circumstances demand.

George then turned Charlie Golf round and headed back to the Waingapu airstrip for a third attempt at landing. The third attempt was as dangerous as the first two and George had to pull out at the last minute. This time, he pulled the joystick back, lifted the aircraft over the trees on the port side, turned a half circle, and manoeuvred Charlie Golf to face directly into the strong headwind.

George was too busy to be scared, but I was terrified. I was hanging on to my seat belt straps with one hand and bracing myself against the console in the crash position with the other. I was holding my breath in sheer terror.

What happened next was nothing short of brilliance.

As Charlie Golf slowed and steadied in the strong headwind, George neatly and expertly guided the aircraft between two radio masts, lifted us over a fence, skimmed the grass roof of the terminal hut and dropped Charlie Golf down on the grass apron that ran between the runway and the hut. We rolled to a shuddering halt within a distance of about 230ft (70 metres).

The relief and elation was indescribable. My nerves were totally shot, but I was immensely proud of the way George got us out of an extremely dangerous predicament.

As we climbed out of the Beagle Terrier, we were immediately surrounded by men, women and children from the local village staring at us with mouths agape. The airport manager thankfully spoke English, so we explained to him our reason for landing. In the meantime, we gave up trying to keep the fifty or so onlookers away from Charlie Golf.

After a short while, the Chief of Police arrived with the Garuda agent and we retired to the grass hut to discuss the purchasing of fuel. It was agreed that George would pay in traveller's cheques. Coffee was served and Charlie Golf was refuelled. All the while, the crowd of curious locals smiled and laughed as they watched us through the windows and doors.

The airport manager then kindly suggested we spend the night in the spare hut behind the airstrip. The hut was a single room with an earthen floor, two camp beds, two pillows, and a table. There was no glass in the window openings. We were provided with a storm lamp and a bucket of cold water with which to wash.

We were visited by several of the airstrip staff and their family members. After they left, we were kindly given a meal of rice, fried chicken in coconut oil and a vegetable soup mixture to pour over the rice. Because his mouth and gums were still giving him trouble, George couldn't eat and, in order not to insult our host, he discretely disposed of his meal into the surrounding long grass. I, on the other hand, found the meal to be quite palatable.

We donned our long-sleeved shirts and trousers and lit a couple of mosquito rings before settling down for the night. I think I must have been allergic to the insecticide in the vapour, as I woke at midnight with an asthma attack. When I could breathe easily again, I dozed off dreaming of Darwin, now only two more flights away, and anticipating the telegrams we would send if and when we finally got there.

Chapter 23

Portuguese Timor

More conflict and curiosity

Sunday 13 October 1968
Waingapu–Dili, Portuguese Timor
Time of departure: 23.52 GMT Flying time: 4hrs 40mins
Flying conditions: Hot, some cloud, poor visibility. Wind direction and velocity: n/a.

I woke at 4.00am, washed in the bucket of cold water, then woke George. The two of us carried our gear over to Charlie Golf and prepared the aircraft for take-off. We then returned to the hut where we were given a very adequate breakfast of bread and coffee. As we were leaving, George emptied his pockets and gave our host all the Indonesian currency we had left.

I climbed into the cockpit and the two of us went through the familiar procedure of starting up. This time though, the Gypsy Major engine refused to start. George tried every trick in the book to get Charlie Golf to tick over, but to no avail.

After opening up the cowling and tinkering with the engine, George discovered that a screw had come loose in the Impulse magneto and mangled the internal workings. We were both shocked. Getting stuck on this remote island was just not an option.

Almost believing I was wasting my time, I rummaged through the bag of spare parts in the back of the aircraft and, lo and behold, found a new set of magneto points. George said he knew they were there all the time. He then tried to remove the mangled points. I did the fetching and carrying of different screwdrivers and other implements until at last the old ones were out and the new ones in. Unfortunately, while fitting the new points, he was forced to remove a delicate piece of the workings and as he replaced it he cracked the metal.

Nevertheless, it was the best he could do under the circumstances and, with a crowd of curious Indonesians looking on and with our hearts in our mouths, we went through the procedure of firing up the engine for the second time that morning. Success! Charlie Golf roared into life almost immediately. Yes! Hallelujah! We were on the move again.

Without a moment's hesitation, we taxied on to the grass airstrip and lifted off, waving to the crowd as we rose into the sky.

By this time, it was 8.00am local time and the sun had a sting in it, but, despite the cross wind, Charlie Golf left in a much more dignified manner than when we arrived.

Because of the trouble with the magneto, we decided to alter our route and set course for the Northern Islands with the idea of following the coastlines, rather than risk the direct route over the sea to Dili.

Thankfully, the weather was in our favour again and the scenery was spectacular, but we were still very much on edge.

Dili appeared on the horizon within our estimated flight times and even though it had a gravel airstrip with a reasonably strong crosswind, it certainly was not as hazardous as Waingapu.

George executed another perfect landing despite the adverse conditions.

We taxied up to the terminal building only to find the place closed down. Gradually, several men appeared and it became quite evident that we were not expected. It was also evident that because it was Sunday we could not get Charlie Golf refuelled until at least 7.00am the following morning.

The police, when they arrived, wanted money for visas before they would allow us to leave the airport. As we didn't have any ready cash, they took our passports instead and told us we would get them back in the morning.

We made Charlie Golf safe and then climbed into the back of the police Jeep to be taken to a hotel. The hotel looked out over the deep blue-green sea and was really quite appealing. We were given a comfortable, reasonably priced room with a veranda that looked out over the water.

The little we had seen of Dili so far reminded us of Spain. Sandy roads, chalk-white, low-roofed houses and gardens full of colourful shrubs and trees, although we were surprised at how few people could speak or understand the English language.

Once settled, George took off to the bar while I washed our very smelly flying clothes.

As I stepped into the shower, I was faced with the biggest and ugliest brown spider I have ever seen. It was sitting on the plastic shower curtain and scared the wits out of me. I tried to get it onto the floor to drown it, but couldn't. George saved the day with a spray can of insecticide.

As we ate a very enjoyable dinner in the hotel dining room, we discussed our onward travel plans and agreed that our best option was to leave for Darwin in the morning.

George's sore mouth was still troubling him, but we both were so tired we fell asleep almost immediately.

—

Monday 14 October
Dili, Indonesia

I woke before the alarm went off and lay quiet feeling quite nervous and excited at what the day ahead might hold for us. We managed to gulp down a quick cup of coffee before the taxi arrived at 6.45am.

We had hoped to get Charlie Golf's tanks filled up with fuel as soon as we got to the airfield, but, as we expected might happen, we were forced to wait for ages for the bowser to turn up. It took so long, in fact, that it ruined our chances of taking off that day.

While we were passing the time at the airport, we noticed there were several Austers parked in the hangar, one of which belonged to the Flying Doctor.

We were also fortunate enough to speak to the chief pilot of Timor Air Transport.

He gave us extremely valuable information and we listened very carefully to his advice about crossing the Timor Sea to Darwin. He also helped me to complete the flight plan and told me that in no circumstances was it to be sent until well after we had commenced our flight. The reason for this was that the Australian Civil Aviation Authority did not permit single-engine aircraft to fly over open water in Australian air space. Should they receive the flight plan before we left, it would have given them the opportunity to refuse us permission to enter Australian air space.

The chief pilot was also kind enough to drive us back to the hotel to dump our luggage and then to the office of the police chief to collect our passports.

Through an interpreter, a police officer demanded over £6 for visas. George told him we were not tourists, but air crew in transit. However, this made no difference. When the discussion started to get heated, it was suggested that we wait until the police chief arrived.

We went over to the hotel for a drink, then about an hour later George went back to see the police chief to retrieve our passports.

He returned looking quite angry and frustrated. Apparently the chief agreed that there was special compensation for crew in transit, but he believed we were tourists and nothing would change his mind. The interpreter again suggested that George come back later.

Back in our hotel room, George asked me to write out an affidavit declaring we were not tourists. He then made himself more presentable and returned to the police chief's office.

He was gone for what seemed like an eternity. When he did get back he was absolutely fuming as the chief had flatly refused to give him our passports unless he paid the £6. George apparently had unwisely made violent threats, but it clearly made no difference. If anything, it hardened the police chief's resolve.

It was when George threatened to get up and leave without the passports that I blew a fuse. I was already on edge about the coming Timor Sea crossing and I just could not understand why George had to push every difference of opinion to the absolute limit. I was shaking with anger, frustration and disappointment over his belligerent attitude towards airport officials and authorities in general. It all seemed so trivial. I just wanted him to pay up and keep the peace so that we could be on our way.

The Timorese pilot who had helped us earlier suggested that we could seek assistance from the Australian Embassy. Then two other Australians, who had been nearby, came over and, on hearing what had taken place, told George that from what they knew of the Timorese police, it would be in his absolute best interest to just pay up and not push the matter any further.

After that I'd had enough, so I went for a walk along the beach to clear my thoughts. Interestingly, I noticed I was being closely followed all the way along the beach and back to the hotel.

Much to my relief, when I got back, George had already been to see the police chief and had retrieved our passports. The diary doesn't indicate if he paid the amount requested, but I suspect he must have.

The rest of the day passed without further ado, but we both clearly recall becoming aware of a rising uneasiness about the atmosphere in Dili. We had noticed as the sun went down that several trucks crowded with young men wearing tank tops, fatigues and headbands were noisily driving up and down the streets. What made us uneasy was the fact that the young men were shouting slogans and waving guns and rifles in the air.

That second night in our hotel we made sure our door was securely locked.

Chapter 24

Australia

Crossing the Timor

Tuesday 15 October 1968
Dili — Darwin, Northern Territory, Australia
Time of departure: 21.07 GMT Flying time: 5hrs 57mins
Flying conditions: Fair, high cloud, storm clouds mid-flight.
Wind direction and velocity: n/a.

That morning when I woke my stomach was churning. From the very beginning we both knew that the Timor Sea crossing would be the most dangerous flight of the whole trip, especially as there would be no reliable current weather forecast to go by. We both knew that once we set our course for Darwin, there would be no turning back. We were both fully aware that if we went down in the sea, there was no hope of rescue, whatever the circumstances. We knew that if we did end up in the water, our greatest fear would be the sharks. We both knew nothing would stop us trying, because we believed Charlie Golf could do it.

By the time we got to the airport, I was almost sick with nerves, but George appeared much calmer.

Silently and carefully we prepared Charlie Golf for the trip.

For good measure, George decided to put oil in the engine mid-flight. To do this, he fixed a flexible pipe to the cowling filler inlet using a radiator hose clamp. The pipe was then fed through the window into the cockpit and the end stuffed with a cloth to stop the engine fumes from seeping in. We made sure all the fuel tanks, including the newly fitted spare in the rear, were reading full. George checked to ensure the apparatus for in-flight refuelling was also aboard. We filled the plastic container with avgas and made the cockpit ready for me to have it on my knee until required during the flight.

Finally, we donned the life jackets. This was the first and last time we used them throughout our entire journey.

The preparations and final aircraft checks completed, I climbed into my seat, while George swung the propeller and primed the engine. Charlie Golf immediately roared into life as if it too was eager to get moving.

Our strategy for the first section of the trip was to avoid the climb over the mountains and to fly low along the coast to Baucau. This tactic would use up less fuel.

Navigation was accurate and we overflew Baucau airstrip only two minutes later than the predicted time. George then turned onto the new heading that took us through the valley to the south coast.

As we crossed the coastline and headed out to sea, we looked pointedly at each other, confirming our final commitment and resolve. Although reasonably calm, the sea quickly lost its greeny-blue colours and turned to inky black.

Our strategy for the sea crossing was to stay out of the prevailing winds as much as possible by flying low while maintaining the prescribed compass heading. This meant we travelled about 1000ft above sea level.

Then, about thirty minutes out and the Timorese coast disappearing behind us, for some unknown reason George decided to check the magnetos in flight. He had never done this before, but he later explained that he was suddenly aware of a change in the beat and pitch of the engine. What he discovered was that the problem magneto with the makeshift repair was working alright, but the other magneto, the supposedly good one, was stuffed.

George looked grave and I went to jelly. We looked at each other again, nodded, and that said it all. We plodded on.

The mid-air refuelling procedure was conducted without a hitch and the belly tank was once again full. Having the plastic container on my lap whilst wearing the lifejacket meant I was somewhat squashed and so it was a great relief to get rid of the empty container into the space behind me. I was then able to wriggle my legs and get some feeling back into my buttocks.

We estimated that after about two-and-a-half hours flying, we had reached the point of no return. Every minute seemed like an hour and at times I found myself holding my breath.

Then the generator warning light came on. This had never happened before either. George gave the mechanism under the control panel a hefty knock. The light went out and then came on again. After a couple more hefty knocks that failed to fix the problem, George just switched off the battery connection. He prescribed to the theory out of sight, out of mind.

Well beyond the point of no return, we encountered more problems. Black thunder-clouds were sitting right across our flight path. Carefully scanning the scene before us, we decided that the clouds looked least ominous on our starboard side. As such, George turned Charlie Golf ninety degrees and flew along the front of the clouds until we found a gap that appeared to stretch far enough to enable us to duck under and come out the other side. We carefully timed the deviation from our pre-determined compass heading down to the last second. Having decided the hole in the cloud was big enough for us to get through, George turned Charlie Golf back onto the correct compass heading. As soon as we broke through the bad weather and had blue skies overhead, George reversed the procedure and turned Charlie Golf ninety degrees to port, ensuring we flew along the cloud face with the exact timing as before. I had my eyes on the watch and, when I gave the signal, we turned once more onto the pre-determined compass heading. This was all done with a mixture of judgement and guesswork. We had absolutely no indicators other than the compass to tell us if we were back on the correct course.

Fortunately, we encountered no more bad weather, but the next two hours were still extremely emotionally gruelling.

Shortly after the bad weather episode, we topped up the engine with oil in much the same way as we did the fuel, which is, pouring oil from a can down the pipe and into the engine itself. We then replaced the rag to keep the fumes at bay.

The rest of the time was spent silently staring at the horizon and listening intently to the constant rhythm of that Gypsy Major engine. If the pistons missed a beat, which they did on occasion, my heart also missed a beat.

Then, through the distant haze, I saw what looked like a thin, grey line on the horizon.

My first thought was that I was imagining things and that it was probably a mirage caused by the afternoon heat haze, so I purposely looked out the side window and watched the Timor Sea pass under us. I then glanced over at George and noticed he appeared to be focusing on the horizon. I dared to look again and this time my insides leapt and I almost gasped out loud. There was no doubt. The mirage was getting bigger.

I checked my watch and, according to the timing of our flight plan, we should have been approaching Melville Island by now.

Absolutely elated, George and I whooped with joy as the

thin, grey line on the horizon slowly changed first to a long, sandy-coloured strip and then to green-covered land. It was Melville Island.

I reckoned we were approximately two nautical miles off course and four minutes over the estimated time of arrival. We could hardly believe our success.

After checking the map and calculating the fuel situation, we made the decision that we would overfly Melville Island and head straight into Darwin. We understood it would be cutting things fine, but being only fifty nautical miles out, we were again prepared to take the risk.

The final section of the flight was over Beagle Gulf. We felt this was a good omen and, besides, the sea was now dotted with frigates and shipping vessels, so we reasoned our chances of a sea rescue, should the circumstances arise, had increased tenfold.

As we approached Darwin air space, George called up air traffic control on the given frequency. Much to our relief, the radio transmitter did not let us down and we picked up the Darwin signal loud and clear.

It was blatantly obvious that Darwin control had not yet received our flight plan as they asked us to once again identify our call sign and state our position. I recall that conversation clearly as George repeated, 'I say again, this is Golf Alpha Sierra Charlie Golf, en route to Australia from the U.K, point of departure Dili; present position, flying over Beagle Gulf with an Australian frigate to starboard.' He was then asked to confirm that Charlie Golf was a single-engine aircraft and that we had flown from Dili. George's answer, of course, was, 'Affirmative, Charlie Golf is a single-engine Beagle Terrier and point of departure was Dili.'

We realised we were probably in trouble again, but we were too elated to care.

George then requested a straight-in approach as our fuel situation was getting critical. Although air traffic control acknowledged the request, the approach they gave us took us in a wide arc round the airport.

George executed a perfect landing, but as soon as Charlie Golf's wheels hit Australian soil, the following urgent instruction came over the radio; 'Charlie Golf expedite, Charlie Golf expedite, I say again Charlie Golf expedite.'

We were left in no doubt as to the urgency of the situation and, with a commercial jet bearing down on us from behind, George very quickly cleared the runway and headed for the allocated parking bay.

Our actual time of arrival was exactly three minutes over our estimated time of arrival. We felt quite chuffed with that. How could we not be?

As soon as Charlie Golf came to a halt, George was out the door in a flash and dismantling the pipe that went into the cowling. He did not want the authorities to see that improvisation.

As for me, the first thing I did through my tears of sheer joy and relief was to put my forehead against the aircraft's metal cowling and profusely thank Charlie Golf for getting us here. *Terra firma* never felt so good.

We were instructed to report to customs, health and immigration offices as soon as we landed, but, before we walked away from Charlie Golf, a health official arrived, sprayed inside the cabin with insecticide and shut the doors and windows. Then, on our way to the main administration building, we had to walk through a thick, sloppy, wet sponge of presumably the same insecticide.

Next stop was the health desk where we were supplied with malaria prevention tablets and required to fill out various forms. It was such a pleasure to be dealing with westernised, English-speaking officials who immediately put us at ease.

After health, came customs and immigration. George had to persuade the customs official that the starter gun was a bona fide piece of safety equipment and not a weapon. Apparently, the fact that it required to be loaded with a cartridge before firing led the officer to believe it was a killing firearm. After conversing with his colleagues and looking through several manuals, we were eventually allowed to keep the starter pistol as long as we signed an affidavit. The officer also fastidiously scraped out all the seeds from the little basket that the Indian doll carried on her head.

We were especially pleased to learn that we were not required to pay import duty on Charlie Golf as we had first anticipated.

Checking in with Immigration wasn't a problem as we already had been granted permanent visas before we left the U.K.

The administrative requirements and form-filling seemed to take forever, but we didn't mind one bit. We were in Australia.

We returned to Charlie Golf just as the ground crew were finished the refuelling. The look on the crew's faces was classic. One of them asked George what the fuel capacity of the aircraft was and, when told, informed us that Charlie Golf had taken about five gallons more than the supposed maximum capacity.

George's response was a cool, 'Well, now you know why we requested a straight-in approach.'

After taxiing Charlie Golf over to the designated hangar, another check of the magnetos revealed that one was functioning alright, while the other was completely "stuffed". George said he would arrange to have it repaired before we headed south to Adelaide.

While the administrative requirements were being processed,

one of the health officials, Gordon Wood, kindly invited us to spend our time in Darwin with himself and his wife. We were very pleased to accept his offer and arranged to meet him later at the Darwin Flying Club.

As George made his way to the club to meet Gordon I wandered over to the airport manager's office to check if there was any mail for us. I was then referred to the operations desk. I couldn't believe my eyes when I was presented with a large bundle of mail. I learned that my dad had written directly to the officer requesting that he keep all the mail addressed to us for when we arrived in Darwin. Sobbing with emotion, I ran back to the Flying Club to share the letters with George.

There was correspondence from almost every family member and all our close friends. The congratulatory and caring sentiments were overwhelming and I laughed and cried over each and every letter. Even George was somewhat overcome with all the good wishes.

Our next task was to send telegrams to both sides of the family back in Scotland and to my brother and his family in Adelaide, giving them the wonderful news that we had at long last arrived in Darwin safe and well.

Gordon duly arrived at the Flying Club as arranged and we accompanied him in his car through Darwin to his home. On first impression, we liked what we saw of Darwin — very spacious, wide streets and homes with large, lush, green gardens.

When we got to Gordon's house, George and I both had a much needed shower. While we waited for Gordon's wife, Yvonne, to get home from work, we made a cursory start to plotting our route down the middle of Australia to Adelaide.

We found Yvonne to be a bundle of joyous energy with a very happy and infectious disposition. When she took me shopping to the local supermarket, it all felt surreal. I found it hard to comprehend that at long last I was in Australia. Everything seemed so much like being back home.

That night, we ate our BBQ steaks with salad and talked and laughed until it was quite late. We learned that Gordon and Yvonne had come from South Australia to Darwin to work because the remuneration was much better.

It had been an extremely demanding day, but I couldn't have been happier. Before falling asleep, I read through all those wonderful letters one more time.

Wednesday 16 October
Darwin, Northern Territory

I woke up to a beautiful, warm, sunny morning, thinking about the folks back home. I would have loved to have seen their faces when they received the telegrams we sent.

I was treated to breakfast in bed, while George returned to the airport to see to the magneto problem and to revalidate the fuel carnet.

Having the house to myself for the morning, I used the time to catch up on all the necessary chores, like washing clothes, updating the diary and writing letters and postcards.

At some point, George telephoned to tell me to get ready to go into town. Apparently, he had agreed for us to be interviewed by a reporter at the newspaper office in Darwin.

George also told me that the magneto drop was caused by a faulty spark plug and that he had easily fixed the problem. The fuel carnet, however, probably wouldn't be available until the following day.

Prior to keeping our appointment with the reporter and photographer, we wandered round the main shopping area taking in the sights and smells of Darwin.

The ensuing interview was no different to the many we had given before. So when we were finished, George and I went to a local hotel for a cool beer.

To us, the bar of the hotel was like a set straight out of a western movie — wooden floors, steps up off the street to a veranda, swing doors and the bar lined with jackeroos wearing jeans, open-neck shirts with rolled-up sleeves, spurred boots and wide-brimmed hats. We later learned that the hats were the traditional Aussie akubras. All were drinking ice-cold beers. We were fascinated and watched with quiet amusement.

Back at Gordon and Yvonne's, we thoroughly enjoyed a meal of fish and chips and, like the previous evening, laughed and talked the night away.

Because the fuel carnet had not yet materialised, we made the decision to spend another day in Darwin and to head south on Friday.

—

Thursday 17 October
Darwin, Northern Territory

As our hosts were both at work, we lazed around for most of the morning before George kept a previously made appointment with a dentist to have his gums seen to.

Apparently, the dentist filed a tooth down a little, painted a substance on his gums and suggested that he see another dentist as soon as he got to Adelaide.

George also brought a newspaper back with him and we were quite pleased at the finished article that was published. The headlines read, *Wilbur and Orville had nothing on this! WRIGHT PARTNERS; the honeymoon is over.* A large photograph of George and I sitting in Charlie Golf with our headsets on accompanied the article. The photograph was one that had been taken in Edinburgh the day we left.

Throughout the afternoon we received several telephone calls. One was from the Shell oil company advising us that they were holding a letter that enabled us to purchase fuel for Charlie Golf on credit.

The other calls were from the local post office informing us that there were numerous telegrams for us waiting to be collected. One from the Wright family read, *Congratulations on your great feat what kept you.*

The other was from my brother David asking when we expected to get into Adelaide as a radio station wanted to book us for an interview. We thought it best to wait 'til we got to Alice Springs before sending off an estimated arrival time for Adelaide.

That night, Yvonne and I retired reasonably late leaving George and Gordon getting quite drunk on a bottle of whisky.

I wasn't too happy and was rather disappointed as we had planned to get up at 4.00am to resume our travels to Adelaide.

—

Friday 18 October

Darwin–Daly Waters, Northern Territory

Time of departure: 20.43 GMT Flying time: 3hrs 47mins
Flying conditions: Very hot, extreme turbulence. Wind direction and velocity: Not documented.

The alarm woke me at 4.00am, but I dozed off, then jumped out of bed in a panic at 4.30.

Yvonne and Gordon had breakfast with us and then took us to the airport and waited while we filed our flight plan and packed our gear into the aircraft. We waved goodbye to our hosts just as the sun came up and the air traffic controller cleared Charlie Golf for take-off.

Given we were flying at 2000ft and following the road to Daly Waters, navigating was relatively easy. In fact, apart from the turbulence, we found the four-hour trip to be quite tedious, as once clear of Darwin, there wasn't much to see but sand, bush and scrub. We did look for kangaroos, but failed to spot any.

Despite the turbulent conditions, George managed a smooth landing on the Daly Waters airstrip. We refuelled in very good time and, as there was nowhere at the airstrip we could get refreshments, we decided to push on to Tennant Creek. We were back in the air within the hour. That had to be a record turnaround for us. I was beginning to like this country.

Daly Waters–Tennant Creek, Northern Territory

Time of departure: 01.14 GMT Flying time: 2hrs 53mins
Flying conditions: Very hot, extreme turbulence, good visibility. Wind direction and velocity: Not documented.

Travelling from Daly Waters to Tennant Creek was three hours of pure hell. It was burning hot, extremely turbulent and, again, the scenery, to our untrained eye, was nothing but scrub and desert as far as the eye could see. In the heat of the late morning, the flight seemed to take forever.

On the ground again at Tennant Creek, we immediately refuelled Charlie Golf. Then, too hot and tired to try for a third trip in one day, we hired a taxi to take us to a hotel.

Tennant Creek airport was quite plush and modern, whereas the town itself reminded us of the cowboy towns we had seen in movies. The hotel was extremely comfortable with air conditioning and the first thing we did was to have a cool shower and freshen up.

We then went to a cafe and ordered steak, egg and chips and

were presented with a massive plate of food. It was absolutely delicious, but I still couldn't finish it all.

Later in the evening, George took a call from the *Adelaide Advertiser* newspaper reporter seeking the latest information about our flight itinerary.

That night we bedded down at a very reasonable hour and in no time were fast asleep.

—

Saturday 19 October
Tennant Creek, Northern Territory

By 6.00am, we were up dressed and ready for the taxi to arrive and take us to the airport.

As it was already daylight, we packed Charlie Golf, climbed in and made ready for take-off. As we taxied past the flight briefing rooms, I noticed that someone was already working there. Leaving Charlie Golf's engine running, George jumped out and ran over to the building to speak to the officer. He hurried back with the news that we were required to file a flight plan. Armed with the necessary information, he returned to the flight briefing room and duly registered the flight plan to Alice Springs.

He was gone for what seemed like ages. As the engine was still idling, it took very little time to taxi out onto the runway. However, when George carried out the routine magneto check before taking off, the check revealed that once again one of the magnetos was not functioning. This time, nothing George did would clear it and so we had no alternative but to return Charlie Golf to the holding apron.

Out on the apron, George removed the previously faulty spark plug, cleaned it and then fired up the engine. We still had a magneto drop. Becoming increasingly frustrated, he then took out all the sparks plugs, cleaned them, replaced them and then ran another magneto check. Still no success!

By this time, it was obvious that even if we did get it fixed within a reasonable time, it was now too late to consider flying to Alice Springs.

George made the decision to remove all the spark plugs and take them to the local garage to be cleaned.

We walked back to town and I bought sandwiches and sent a telegram to David, while George organised for the mechanic to have the plugs cleaned.

Back at the airstrip and the plugs replaced, George, for the umpteenth time that morning, fired up the Gypsy Major engine and ran a magneto check. Much to our relief, cleaning the spark plugs appeared to fix the problem as both magnetos functioned beautifully.

The rest of the day in Tennant Creek was spent lazing, resting and reading in the cool, comfortable, hotel room. When we did venture out into the searing heat, it was to take a walk through the town and to eat.

Sunday 20 October
Tennant Creek–Alice Springs, Northern Territory

Time of departure: 20.53 GMT Flying time: 3hrs 17mins
Flying conditions: Very hot, visibility good, clear skies. Wind direction and velocity: Not documented.

On rising that morning we repeated the well-rehearsed procedure of the previous day, only this time we walked to the airport.

We filed a flight plan, received all the necessary flight information and then took off. Once again, the weather was extremely hot and the turbulence excessive. My job as navigator was made easy as we followed the road and railway line all the way. However, like our previous flight, the three hours in the air proved to be quite boring until we approached the hills and welcome greenery that signalled Alice Springs. Perhaps we were anxious to get to Adelaide.

In Alice Springs, we learned that the Shell oil representative would have to come from the town to refuel Charlie Golf, so we negotiated to purchase avgas from the Alice Springs Flying Club instead. This saved us a great deal of time and meant we were able to make a second trip to Oodnadatta before night-fall.

We really appreciated the efficiency and civility with which the airport staff managed the necessary administration routines of our flight and we were already beginning to feel quite at home in this country.

Alice Springs–Oodnadatta, South Australia

Time of departure: 01.14 GMT Flying time: 2hrs 51mins
Flying conditions: Very hot, turbulent, good visibility. Wind direction and velocity: Not documented.

As we set course on our way out of Alice Springs airspace, I made my biggest "stuff up" as a navigator. Perhaps I was relaxing too quickly.

In the briefing, I was told to make a right turn out of Alice Springs as there was a danger area to the left. We had, as before, planned to follow the road and railway line. Somehow, there was confusion about turning right or left. I could see the road on my left and assumed we should head in that direction. Of course, as soon as we did, the air traffic controller came over the radio and told us we were heading in the wrong direction. If we wanted to follow the railway line it was on our right. How embarrassing! George was absolutely livid with me and I copped a hefty thump with his fist on the top of my leg for my mistake.

We eventually calmed down, but the rest of the flight was anything but pleasant. The heat and constant turbulence at 1,500ft was proving to be exhausting.

Despite the turbulence, the landing on the Oodnadatta airstrip was very respectable. The Shell oil representative, Mr Pick, who refuelled Charlie Golf, also took us to the only bar in the only hotel in the one street town.

By 6.00pm local time, we had freshened up and cooled off. We spoke to a couple of opal miners while having a drink in the bar. One of them gave me a few small pieces of white opal. Mr Pick then kindly offered to take us for a drive in his dust-covered Land Rover and show us a desert waterhole. During the sightseeing tour, we both noticed what looked like a rifle lying in full view in the back of the vehicle. We weren't quite sure what to make of that.

Flies, or the number thereof, were an absolute pest. They were trying to crawl up our nostrils and get into our eyes and ears. We were fascinated at the number that could stick to the clothes on our back. Not having experienced anything like this before, we found it quite annoying and revolting. Our host just flipped them away with a wave of his hand and didn't seem too perturbed at all.

On returning to the hotel, Mr Pick offered the use of his Land Rover to go to the airstrip in the morning. George accepted with thanks.

As we were preparing to bed down for the night, we discovered the room was infested with beetles. They were everywhere; even in our beds. We weren't very successful at getting rid of them, so eventually we gave up and went to bed. We did not sleep well that night.

—

Monday 21 October
Oodnadatta–Leigh Creek, South Australia

Time of departure: 20.28 GMT Flying time: 2hrs 25mins
Flying conditions: Cooler, strong winds, turbulence. Wind direction and velocity: Not documented.

I lay awake for ages before the alarm went off. This could be the last day of flying and, if all went according to plan, by nightfall we would be in Adelaide with my brother and his family. I was so excited. My nerves were on edge and my stomach was churning.

Before leaving the hotel, we crept into the kitchen and made ourselves a mug of coffee. When we climbed into the Land Rover to make our way back to the airstrip, we were amazed to find the rifle was still positioned in full view on the back seat. Australians seem to be a very trusting people.

Once at the airstrip, we used the telephone to file a flight plan to Leigh Creek, then when Charlie Golf was packed and all was ready, we taxied out onto the airstrip and took off.

The sun was up by this time, but we had a light cloud cover that took the sting out of the sun's heat. We also had unexpected favourable tail winds.

In what seemed like no time at all, we were entering Leigh Creek air space. Once again our equipment failed us and we were unable to make radio contact with Leigh Creek air traffic control. However, we kept vigilant visual flight and landed on the runway without any major problems. It turned out that Leigh Creek air traffic control was also unable to receive our signal. As we were refuelling Charlie Golf, an airport technician tried to locate the fault in the radio transmitter, but couldn't find anything wrong with it.

As a safe-guard, we requested and received permission to fly into Parafield Airfield without a functioning radio transmitter. We felt confident our request would not be refused.

The weather report we got for the trip to Parafield did not look too promising, so we took off knowing that we would be kept busy and the trip would most probably be an uncomfortable one.

—

Leigh Creek–Parafield, Adelaide, South Australia

Time of departure: 00.13 GMT Flying time: 4.00hrs
Flying conditions: Sand storm, severe turbulence. Wind direction and velocity: Not documented.

As soon as we were airborne, we established loud and clear radio contact with Leigh Creek. Much to our relief, the temperamental radio transmitter had decided to kick in again.

Our last trip started with a reasonable tail wind. Then about ten minutes south of Leigh Creek, we encountered a dense sandstorm accompanied by extreme turbulence. Avoiding the high ground, George managed to skirt round the edge of the storm, but with the minimal visibility and turbulence, he had his work cut out for him. We later discovered that the sandstorm had stripped the paint off the metal leading edges of Charlie Golf's wooden propeller.

Once the visibility improved, I guided him back to the road that we planned to follow as a tracking guide into Parafield.

About 100nautical miles out of Adelaide, we turned left to follow the road down the South Australian coast and immediately noticed a change in weather conditions. It was much cooler and we had a head wind.

As we travelled down the homeward run, our moods lifted considerably. We laughed at the fact that some of the cars on the road seemed to be moving faster than we were. On our port side the high terrain that was Flinders Ranges appeared quite picturesque in a blue-grey haze.

Our spirits were high. My excitement and anticipation was palpable.

We located Dublin and, as instructed, turned to follow the coastline to Port Adelaide.

Despite our previous radio problems Parafield Airfield air traffic control came over loud and clear.

George was asked if we had another light aircraft in sight ahead of us. He replied, 'Affirmative. We have aircraft in sight.'

We were then instructed to follow the Victor aircraft onto finals. Despite the tense anticipation, the elation and the emotion, George faultlessly put Charlie Golf down on the grass strip of Parafield Airfield.

We had flown 12,531nautical miles in 168.5 hours over a period of four months and two days.

With huge grins, we hugged and congratulated each other.

Tears were streaming down my face as we taxied over to the entourage of television, radio and newspaper reporters, airport officials and, of course, my brother David and my sister-in-law, Chris.

They said we wouldn't get here, so we did.

Epilogue

During the weeks following our emotional touchdown at Adelaide Parafield Airfield on that day in October 1968, George and I gave many media interviews, including a short appearance on a Channel 9 television program, *Adelaide Tonight,* compered by Kevin Crease. As was to be expected, the media gradually lost interest and we quietly faded from the spotlight. We did not receive any remuneration for these interviews.

My older brother, David, and sister-in-law, Chris, kindly opened their home to us until we found our own apartment close by.

Within a very short period of time, George and I decided that Australia was the right place for us to settle. In particular, we loved and appreciated the wide, clean streets of Adelaide, the friendliness and relaxed "she'll be right" attitude of its people, and, of course, the perfect weather.

George enquired into studying for a Commercial Pilot's licence, but, unfortunately for us at that time, the cost was prohibitive. We didn't have that sort of money. He also wanted to continue on and fly Charlie Golf to Perth to see if our options were better in the west. However, I flatly refused to get back in the air. I well and truly had enough of air travel and navigating and had no desire to make one more trip. I did, however, encourage George to go on his own, but he made the decision not to.

Members of the Royal Aero Club of Parafield immediately took us under their wing and welcomed us as one of their own.

We made many good friends and for many years enjoyed the social life that association with such a club offered.

As for Charlie Golf, unfortunately, our aircraft was the only asset we had. We had no additional money in the bank to speak of. We could not afford the upkeep, nor could we consider flying as a social pastime. Sadly, Charlie Golf had to be sold and we had to find conventional, paid employment.

The Royal Naval Airbase at Nowra bought Charlie Golf to tow their gliders for trainee pilots. As part of the sale, George was able to negotiate a deal whereby we kept Charlie Golf's propeller. The pitch of the wooden propeller that took us across the world was not deep enough for towing gliders and, as such, the new owners replaced it with a more suitable metal propeller.

Charlie Golf's black, wooden propeller with yellow, metal leading edge, to this day has pride of place on the lounge room wall in George's home.

Unfortunately, we found out many years later that Charlie Golf, while trying to take off with a full load during the hottest part of the day, failed to clear the boundary fence of a New South Wales airstrip and crashed. George eventually traced the metal cowling, bent and dusty, in the back of a farmer's shed.

A very sad ending for such a gutsy aircraft.

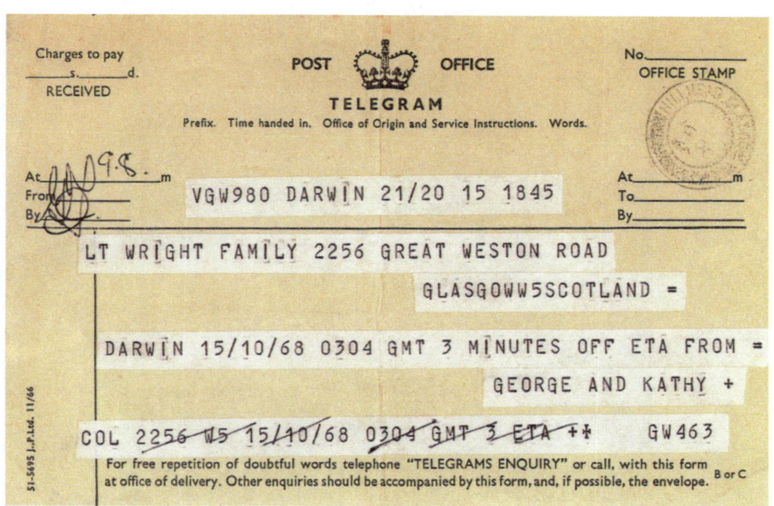

Charges to pay
s. d.
RECEIVED

POST OFFICE
TELEGRAM

No.
OFFICE STAMP

Prefix. Time handed in. Office of Origin and Service Instructions. Words.

At 9.8. m
From
By

At m
To
By

VGW980 DARWIN 21/20 15 1845

LT WRIGHT FAMILY 2256 GREAT WESTON ROAD
GLASGOWW5SCOTLAND =

DARWIN 15/10/68 0304 GMT 3 MINUTES OFF ETA FROM =
GEORGE AND KATHY +

COL 2256 W5 15/10/68 0304 GMT 3 ETA ++ GW463

For free repetition of doubtful words telephone "TELEGRAMS ENQUIRY" or call, with this form at office of delivery. Other enquiries should be accompanied by this form, and, if possible, the envelope. B or C

51-5695 J.,P.Ltd. 11/66

Telegram to Scotland announcing arrival in Darwin

A joyous reunion marks the end of an adventure — Parafield Airfield
L-R George, Kate and David

George demonstrates how he filled the belly tank mid-flight

Charlie Golf's propeller on display

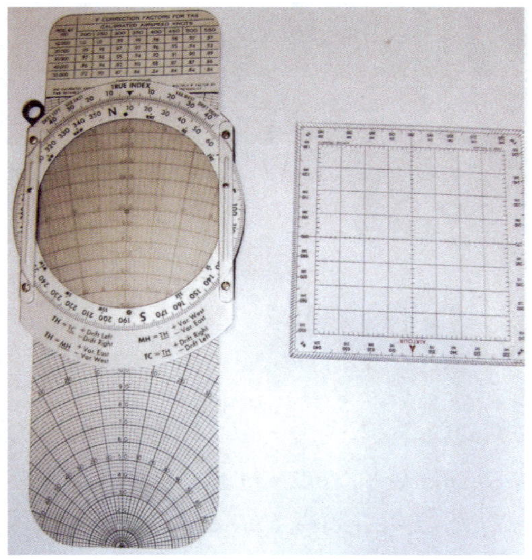

Slide rule and set-square Kate used to plot the compass heading

M.

WED. 19TH JUNE

From		To	Date	n.m.	Gallons
Edinburgh	-	Southend			
Southend	-	Dijon	21.6.68	280 n.m.	28 gallon
Dijon	-	Marseilles	22.6.68	240	24
Marseilles	-	Aighero(Sardinia)	24.6.68	240	24
Aighero	-	Tunis	27.6.68	260	26
Tunis	-	Tripoli (Lybia)	30.6.68	320	32
Tripoli	-	Marble Arch (Lybia)		300	30
Marble Arch	-	Benghazi (Lybia)	1.7.68	170	17
Benghazi	-	El Adem (Lybia)		250	25
El Adem	-	Alexandria (Egypt)	3.7.68	300	30
Alexandria	-	Cairo	4.7.68	100	10
Cairo	-	Hurghad(Egypt)	Beirut 10.7.68	220	22
Hurghad	-	Aqaba(Jordan)	13 7 68	160	16
Aqaba	-	Amman(Jordan)	QATAR 20.7.68	150	15
Amman	-	Badanah(Saudi Arabia)	22.7.68	260	26
Badanah	-	Kaisomah(SaudiArabia)	25.7.68	320	32
Kaisomah	-	Daharan(Saudi Arabia)	1.8.68	230	23
Daharan	-	Aba Dhabi(Tracial Oman)	7.8.68	260	26
Aba Dhabi	-	Sharjah	PC 11.8.68	80	8
Sharjah	-	Jiwani(Pakistan)		350	35
Jiwani	-	Karachi(Pakistan)	PC 14.8.68	300	30
Karachi	-	Jamnagar(India)	L 19.8.68	230	23
Jamnagar	-	Ahmadabad(India)	PC 21.8.68	150	15
Ahmadabad	-	Indore(India)	L 2.9.68	180	19
Indore	-	Jubbulpore(India)	PC 3.9.68	250	25
Jubbulpore	-	Darima(India)		200	20
Darima	-	Ranchi(India)	PC 21.8.68	120	12
Ranchi	-	Calcutta(India)	PC 29.8.68	200	20
Calcutta	-	Chittagong	PC 3.9.68	200	20
Chittagong	-	Akyab(Burma)		200	20
Akyab	-	Rangoon	5.9.68	280	28
Rangoon	-	Tavoy		200	20
Tavoy	-	Mergui		110	11
Mergui	-	Phuket		300	30
Phuket	-	Butterworth		200	20
Butterworth	-	Kuala Lumpur		160	16
Kuala Lumpur	-	Singapore		180	18
Singapore	-	Singkep		110	11
Singkep	-	Palesbang		150n.m.	15 gallons
Palesbang	—	Djakarta		240	24
Djakarta	-	Semerang		220	22
Semerang	-	Surabaya		140	14
Surabaya	-	Soembawa		300	30
Soembawa	-	Flores Riland(provisional)		180	18
Flores Riland	-	Kupang		110	11
Kupang	-	Baucau		250	25
Baucau	-	Bathurst Island Mission (Melville Island)		320	32
Melville Island	-	Darwin		150	15

Original log of planned route from Scotland to Australia, 1968

6-Aug-68	Bhuj	Ahmedabad	165	04.54	1.56	Turbulent with showers, visibility good
10-Aug-68	Ahmedabad	Indore	180	03.32	2.09	Very low cloud, stratus, rain, visibility poor
11-Aug-68	Indore	Nagpur	240	03.31	3.01	Very low cloud, stratus, turbulent
17-Aug-68	Nagpur	Raipur	170	01.31	2.05	Very low cloud, tail wind, fair visibility
18-Aug-68	Raipur	Jamshedpur	270	04.47	3.19	Low cloud, showers, thunder, warm
20-Aug-68	Jamshedpur	Calcutta	130	01.34	2.32	Cloud and showers
31-Aug-68	Calcutta — India	Chittagong — East Pakistan	190	00.13	2.22	Misty, poor visibility
4-Sep-68	Chittagong	Cox's Bazar	50	02.01	1.11	Low cloud, dense sea mist at ground level
5-Sep-68	Cox's Bazar — East Pakistan	Akyab — Burma	95	02.20	1.18	Low cloud, stratus, poor visibility
5-Sep-68	Akyab — Burma	Rangoon	300	05.01	4.21	Low cloud, thunderstorms, showers,
6-Sep-68	Rangoon	Moulmein	270	03.27	4.07	Severe rain storm
7-Sep-68	Moulmein	Mergui	250	02.20	3.43	Thunderstorms, low cloud, poor visibility
8-Sep-68	Mergui -Burma	Phuket — Thailand	260	00.55	3.52	Few rain showers, clear visibility, turbulent
12-Sep-68	Phuket — Thailand	Penang — Malaysia	220	03.05	3.08	Warm, few low clouds, moderate visibility
12-Sep-68	Penang	Kuala Lumpur	160	07.49	2.27	Hot, clear skies, haze, poor visibility
17-Sep-68	Kuala Lumpur — Malaysia	Singapore — Singapore	175	02.27	2.24	Cloudy, good visibility, turbulent, cool
10-Oct-68	Singapore — Singapore	Palembang -Sumatra	260	23.00	3.45	Isolated thundershowers, poor visibility
10-Oct-68	Palembang — Sumatra	Djakarta — Indonesia	235	03.49	3.14	Clear skies, good visibility, hot
11-Oct-68	Djakarta	Surabaja	360	01.02	5.09	Excellent conditions, some cloud cover
11-Oct-68	Surabaja	Bali DenPasar	200	07.45	2.31	Good conditions, rainstorms at destination
12-Oct-68	Bali DenPasar	Waingapu	310	00.05	5.08	Strong X-wind on runway, 20knots, turbulent
13-Oct-68	Waingapu — Indonesia	Dilli — Portuguese Timor	330	23.52	4.41	Hot, little cloud, poor visibility
15-Oct-68	Dili — Portuguese Timor	Darwin — Australia	413	21.07	5.57	Storm mid-channel, high cloud, sea mist
18-Oct-68	Darwin	Daly Waters	280	20.43	3.47	Very hot, ext turbulence
18-Oct-68	Daly Waters	Tennant Creek	208	01.14	2.53	Very hot, ext turbulent, good visibility
20-Oct-68	Tennant Creek	Alice Springs	275	20.53	3.17	Ext hot, good visibility, clear skies
20-Oct-68	Alice Springs	Oodnadatta	241	01.14	2.51	Ext hot, visibility good, turbulent
21-Oct-68	Oodnadatta	Leigh Creek	245	20.28	2.25	Cooler, strong winds, turbulent
21-Oct-68	Leigh Creek	Parafield — Adelaide	290	00.13	4.01	Hot Sand storm, severe turbulence
			12531		168.5	
		TOTALS	**12,531 n/miles**		**168.5 hours**	

Copy of actual log Scotland to Australia

EDINBURGH, SCOTLAND TO ADELAIDE, AUSTRALIA 1968

DATE	FROM	TO	NAUTICAL MILES	TAKE/OFF GMT	FLIGHT TIME HOURS	FLYING CONDITIONS
19-Jun-68	Edinburh — Scotland	Brough — England	165	07.37	4.01	Low cloud-thunderstorms-sea mist
19-Jun-68	Brough	Southend	136	14.34	2.26	Sea mist, low cloud
21-Jun-68	Southend	Calais — France	145	11.11	1.57	Thunderstorms, sleet, rain
22-Jun-68	Calais — France	Dijon Longvic	255	11.41	3.09	Drizzle, mist then clear skies
22-Jun-68	Dijon Longvic	Marseille	231	16.17	4.05	Good visibility — very strong head wind
24-Jun-68	Marseille	Ajaccio — Corsica	221	11.03	2.48	Strong Gusty winds, haze, good visibility
24-Jun-68	Ajaccio — Corsica	Alghero — Sardinia	82	16.25	1.03	Gusty winds, sea haze
25-Jun-68	Alghero — Sardinia	Cagliari	110	10.58	1.46	Ext. Hot, turbulent over mountains,
27-Jun-68	Cagliari — Sardinia	Tunis — Tunisia	155	08.10	1.59	Hot, sea haze on horizon
29-Jun-68	Tunis	Djerba	180	05.25	2.52	Ext poor visibility, desert haze
29-Jun-68	Djerba — Tunisia	Tripoli — Libya	140	10.56	1.44	Dust, poor visibility, horizon haze
1-Jul-68	Tripoli	Ras Lanuf	320	08.18	4.06	Hot, dense sand haze
1-Jul-68	Ras Lanuf	Benghazi	180	13.16	2.19	Hot, humid ,stratus
2-Jul-68	Benghazi	El Adem	240	08.46	3.24	Turbulent with strong down drag
3-Jul-68	El Adem — Libya	Alexandria — Egypt	300	07.27	4.23	Ext hot, good visibility
4-Jul-68	Alexandria	Cairo	130	06.37	1.45	Haze, poor visibility
10-Jul-68	Cairo — Egypt	Beirut — Lebanon	360	03.10	5.21	Poor visibility, low cloud along coast
13-Jul-68	Beirut — Lebanon	Damascus — Syria	62	08.57	2.01	Visibility fair, no air for climbing
13-Jul-68	Damascus — Syria	Amman — Jordan	196	13.37	2.53	Turbulent, haze, poor climbing conditions
17-Jul-68	Amman — Jordan	Badanah — Saudi Arabia	281	03.15	3.59	Ext hot, fair visibility
18-Jul-68	Badanah	Qaisumah	325	03.42	3.34	Burning hot, poor visibility
19-Jul-68	Qaisumah	Ras Tanura	230	02.07	4.32	Humid, strong head wind
19-Jul-68	Ras Tanura	Dhahran	27	14.14	0.31	Very poor visibility, humid, cooler
20-Jul-68	Dhahran -Saudi Arabia	Doha — Qatar	97	02.37	1.38	Ext humid, misty
21-Jul-68	Doha — Qatar	Sharjah — Trucial States	245	02.08	3.42	Very hot, wind changeable
25-Jul-68	Sharjah	Sharjah	104	01.58	2.09	Low cloud
26-Jul-68	Sharjah	Dibba	52	03.33	0.53	Humid, cooler with cloud cover
26-Jul-68	Dibba — Trucial States	Jiwani — Pakistan	300	05.12	4.34	Poor visibility, cooler
27-Jul-68	Jiwani	Karachi	310	04.29	4.01	Low cloud, sea fog
3-Aug-68	Karachi — Pakistan	Bhuj — India	180	05.53	2.21	Bad visibility, tracking conditions poor

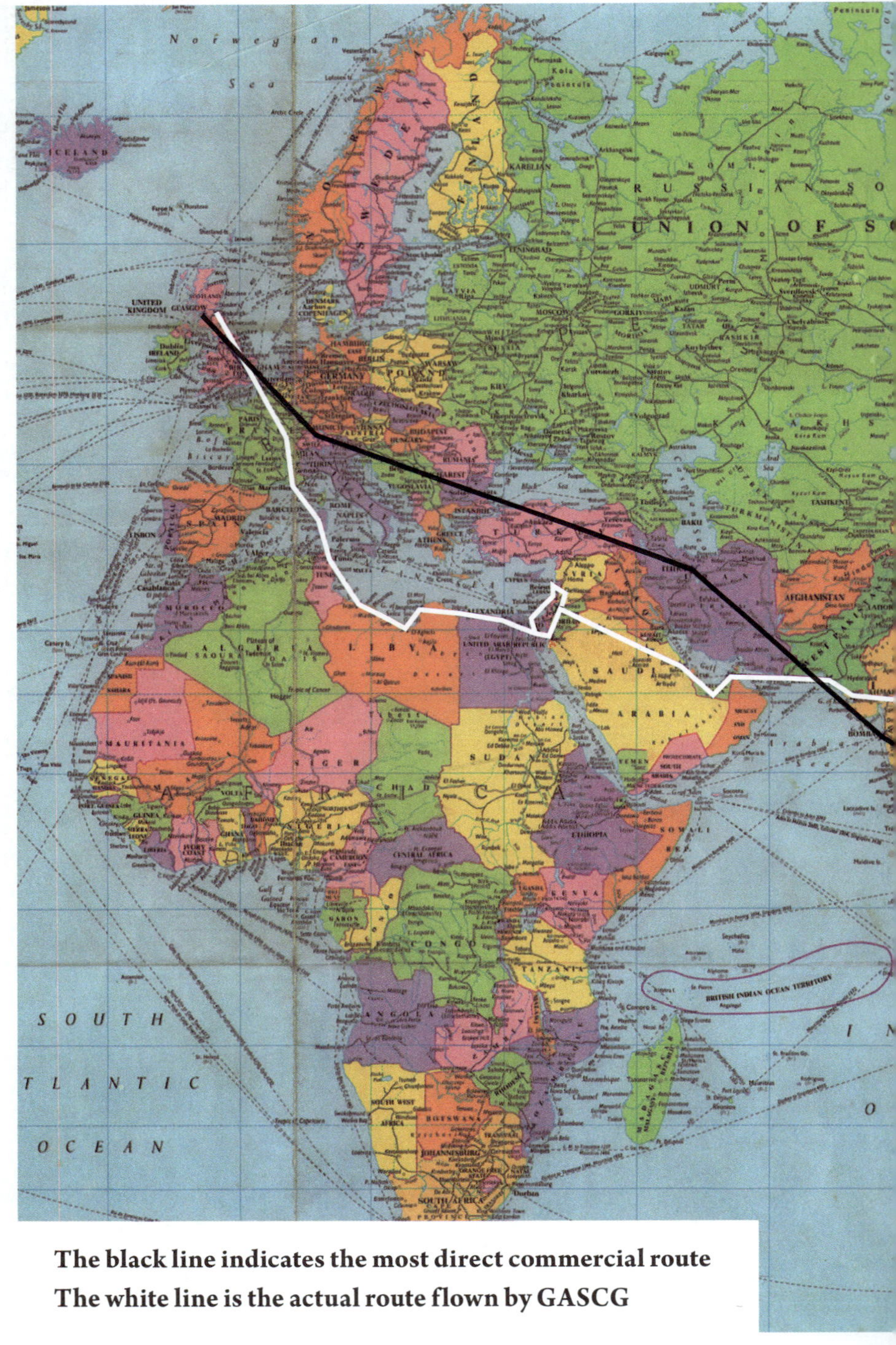

The black line indicates the most direct commercial route
The white line is the actual route flown by GASCG

Copy of the actual 1968 world map used to plot the course from Scotland to Australia

New Releases... also from Sid Harta Publishers

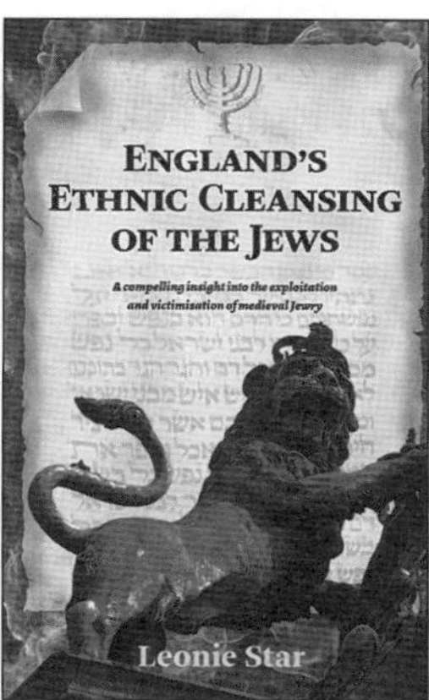

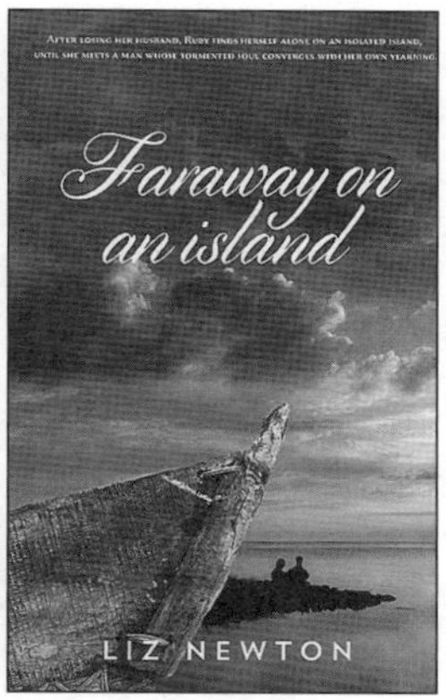

OTHER BEST SELLING SID HARTA TITLES CAN BE FOUND AT

http://sidharta.com.au http://Anzac.sidharta.com

HAVE YOU WRITTEN A STORY?
http://publisher-guidelines.com

Best-selling titles by Kerry B. Collison

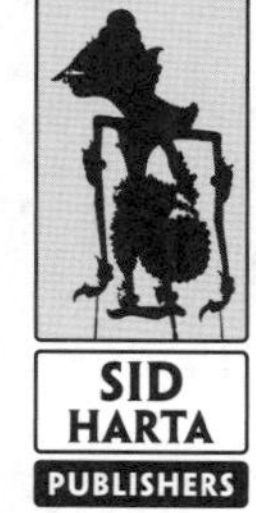

Readers are invited to visit our publishing websites at:
http://sidharta.com.au
http://publisher-guidelines.com/

Kerry B. Collison's home pages:
http://www.authorsden.com/visit/author.
asp?AuthorID=2239
http://www.expat.or.id/sponsors/collison.html
email: author@sidharta.com.au

Purchase Sid Harta titles online at:
http://sidharta.com.au

New Releases... also from Sid Harta Publishers

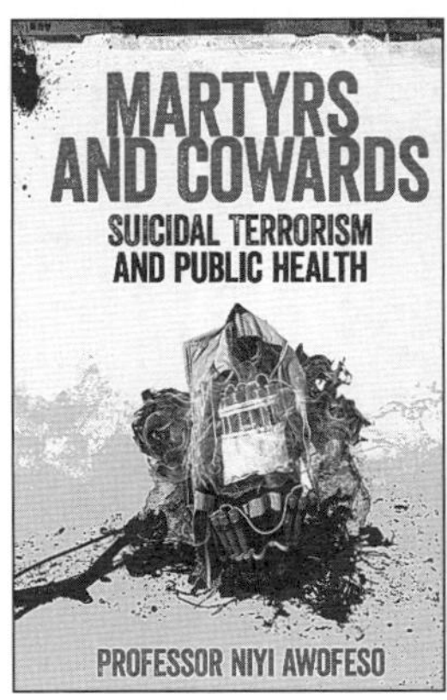

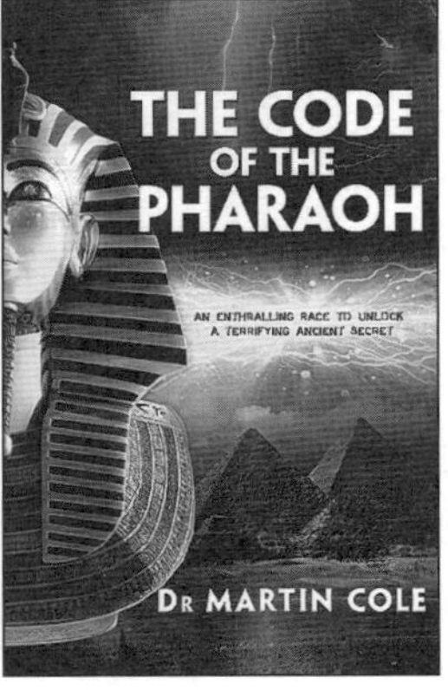

OTHER BEST SELLING SID HARTA TITLES CAN BE FOUND AT

http://sidharta.com.au http://Anzac.sidharta.com

HAVE YOU WRITTEN A STORY?
http://publisher-guidelines.com